LAND, LIGHT, WIND, AND WATER

Prairie Quartet

Elemental Meditations in Four Cycles

Land Sake
The Big Lights
What the Wind S(...)
The Sound of Many Waters

by James Howard Trott

Revised Editions 2009/2015

Oak and Yew Press
Philadelphia

Land, Light, Wind and Water

Prairie Quartet

First edition published privately, in Philadelphia, copyright 1993 James Howard Trott, James Edwards Trott, editor.

Revised Edition, copyright 2009, 2015 James Howard Trott

Land, Light, Wind, and Water is a quartet of meditations on the ancient elements: earth, fire, air and water, as they combine where the northern Great Plains meet the Rocky Mountains.

"The Big Lights" first published by *New Hope International* (23 Gambrel Road, Gee Cross, Hyde, Cheshire, SK 14), England, 1989; Gerald England, editor. Copyright James Howard Trott, 1989.

"Rough Roads" published in *Symphony*, November 1985, Bemerton Press, 57 Raglan Court, Empire Way, Wembley, Middlesex, England (present address; 9 Hamilton Gardens., London, England).

"Moonlight" published in *New Hope International*, Volume 13, Number 6, 1989/90 (address as above).

Dedications of
The Four Cycles
as originally published:

To my Father and Mother who love the land
LANDSAKE

To Roseann, of a higher order of magnitude
THE BIG LIGHTS

To my cousin David Dyrland, who sometimes listens
WHAT THE WIND SAID

In memory of Nancy Ann Long who heard
THE SOUND OF MANY WATERS

CONTENTS

Land Sake

1	Landsake
3	On Ararat
4	The Land
5	Sod Huts
6	Mud
7	Dust
8	Prairie
10	Mirage
11	Agriculture
12	Rough Roads
13	Dirt Roads and Gravel
14	The High Places
15	The Buffalo Jump
16	Gather Stones Together
17	This Is a Desert Place
19	Promised Land

The Big Lights

21	The Big Lights
24	Dawn Light
25	Morning Light
25	Midsummer Sun
27	Summer Clouds
28	Light of Fall
29	Light of Falling Snow
29	Clear Day After Snow
31	Spring Light
32	Storm Light

32	Light Before Hail
33	Two Sides of the Sky
34	Lightning
35	Rainbow Light
36	Fire Light
37	Evening Light
39	Sunset
41	Twilight
42	Reflections
43	Moonlight
44	Starlight
46	The Northern Lights
47	Conclusion

What The Wind Said

49	Unseen Forces
50	Weathervane
51	Winter Wind
53	Wind Chill Factor
54	Chinook
55	After the Chinook
55	I'm Gonna Die
57	Spring Wind
58	Mountain Breeze
59	Big Wind's A-Growin'
60	Storm Wind
62	Wind in the Willows
64	The Four Winds
66	The Windless Times
67	Whirlwind
68	Night Wind
71	Cloud-Driver

71 Windmill
74 Three Persons of the Wind
75 The North Wind's Doorstep
75 Profits Shall Become Wind
77 Fall Wind
78 What the Wind Said
80 Things in the Wind

The Sound of Many Waters

83 Come to the Waters
84 Spring Water
86 Mountain Snows
87 Cloudbursts
88 By the Rivers of Babylon
90 The Rain In the Leaves
91 Rivulets
91 As the Deer Longs for the Flowing Stream
92   Shonkin Creek
94 The Dipper
95 Beaver Dams and Muskrat Tunnels
96 Lakes
98 Dry Year
98 Farm Laborer Drowned
99 Hebgen Lake 1959
100 Navigable River
102 Late-Watch Song of a Land-Locked Sailor
103 Kingfisher
103 Muddy Waters
104 Triple Divide (Rivers Come Dovm)
107 Surfaces and Bends
107 Steamboat
110 Aquatic Origins

112 River as Cynic
114 The Return
114 Great Heart the Ocean
116 Lacrimae

Land, Light, Wind and Water

LANDSAKE

Τα κακως τρέφοντα χωρί ἀνδρείους ποιεί.
("The country which is cultivated with difficulty
produces brave men .")
-- Menander

I. Landsake

"My land!... for land's sake!"
Old exclamations of the parched pioneers,
Rooted in the dubious belief that this of the ancient elements-
This heavy, dark, inert, most stable one is ours.
(Humbly we admit it is the lowest of the four,
But suitable to our humor.)

The modern jokes about superstition and a man-centered
    universe,
With stars rotating about the earth are topsy-turvy
Whose universe is anthropocentric, oh you worshippers at
    mirrors ?
In the medieval view the lowest sphere was at the center;
The higher celestial harmonies were found at further
    removes.
We Westerners have resurrected the scheme --
Nothing near us is of great moment.

But earth, land: forty, eighty or a hundred and sixty acres
To own, to homestead, looked attainable

Land, Light, Wind and Water

And became everyman's dream, every woman's dream,
(A chance for woman to be free
To buy back the garden with the sweat of her brow.)
" But landsake, what have we got ourselves into ! "

Yes, for land's sake hands grew hard, backs bent,
Hearts weighed down and minds sometimes broken.
Many proved up on their land, but proved little
Because drought years and depression years stripped all but
    a few,
Took away their land and put it in the hands of others.
(In the hands of government, mostly, although sometimes
It went to businessmen, or luckier or better farmers.)

But as many as had fingernails stayed --
On their semi-arid, dust-blown acres, or if not,
Stayed near the land, in town, beginning small businesses :
Blacksmiths, bakeries, cafés and groceries, machinery shops,
Bars, insurance sales, government jobs, and odd work --
For what reason, unknown to them ?
For the land's sake.

The broad land, the wide land, the rolling land owned them,
Had plowed their souls and planted there, proved up,
Put in roots and claimed its acres, its heart-acres :
The expanse, the contours, the colors, the weather,
The smells, the seasons, the creak of leather
And the skirr of wind, the brightness of the lights,
The sound of water and the star-strewn nights --
So here we are, timid third and fourth generations
For the land's sake, for landsake !

Land, Light, Wind and Water

II. *On Ararat*

Arid Ararat, scene of recent years' stir
Over remnants of some structure discovered up there
Reputedly of gopher-wood, matching the dimensions
Of the ark prescribed to Noah, needs no mention here
Except as a type, the archetype of this high, dry land
Where so many arks grounded, new covenants began.

For these, too, were fleeing the pollutions of civilization,
The hard-lots and harlotry at the end of a nation --
The other end, by the many waters, encompassed by floods --
Looking for a clean start as the Conestoga scuds.

Close kin and family reacted as Mrs. Noah may have,
" What in tarnation would make a person do that ! "
But she ended up going along
(Unlike Mrs. Job, whose advice was not unlike what Noah's
    friends said.)
They took the whole world with them, the surviving world,
And under a rainbow, began what seemed brand new.

> *Oh don't you remember sweet Betsy from Pike*
> *Who crossed the great desert with her lover Ike*
> *With two yoke of oxen, a large yellow dog*
> *A tall Shanghai rooster and one spotted hog.*

And Noah was strict with his sons -- long, hard years
Of doing what the old man said as crazy as it all sounded --
So that they were welded to him by habit,
But also by the criticism of his public.
Nonetheless, tons of manure later, in the new land,
They reintroduced the snake into paradise.

But think of the time on the boat itself --
The deep delight of the in-between, the leaving and going,
And the not-knowing-where, the uncertainty about
    somewhere ;
Wind and rain in their faces; the animal noises and chores ;
The close-knitting labor of the community
With no other living soul on earth.

Then they arrived. And here we are tasting
Not the fresh start of the forty days and nights only,
But also the fruit of the weedy new transgressions --
When God realized that sin was almost an organ
In his fallen image, his dearest and most destructive
Creature. The third time the dove stayed away.

Ararat, the peak above the arid Turkish plains,
Stands over there above our struggling ranches and farms.
At this end of destruction the only difference is
There aren't enough of us to build Babel, Sodom or
    Gomorrah.
And we are too caught up in coaxing life out of arid plains
To need destroying with a flood.
Not to mention, God promised.

III. *The Land*

    The land drew these wild-eyed romantics,
    Dirt to own, soil out of toil
    To make a man royal in a small way,
    But the original way -- subduing some earth.

Yet the land defeats us --
Lays out the objective reality of our insignificance,
Challenges us to the empirical formula :
Infinity plus zero equals infinity --
The land remains, but what remains of us ?
Oh, you fools of city-dwellers, you see too little earth :
No vastness but the towers of your turning.
You have forgotten the ruins
Choked in jungles, blasted by sand
And buried under layers of other hasty dwellings.
The land draws and conquers,
Builds up and breaks down,
And only welcomes us,
When we consent again to be made soil.

IV. Sod Huts

Our nomad fathers built sod huts,
Laying the dirt prematurely above their heads,
The grass fading, flowers that fell.
They were humble interlopers,
Tentative in their habitations,
Wishing neither to anger
The unknown powers ruling the strange land,
Nor invest more than they must :
Against a sudden departure.
The grass roots, torn up, cannot have dangled
More uncertainly than our fathers',
Their dusty long legs
Recently pulled from some thin soil

Yet sod huts became their homes :
Places of love, birth, labor, eating,
Mirth, sleep, prayer, and death.
None stayed in them long ;
For at first thrill of permanence
They built better dwellings,
Roofed with something more lasting.
Yet do our nomad fathers sleep
In withered-grass sod huts tonight.

V. Mud

Out of mud He made --
But you interupt me:
You ask, " He who !"
Ev Aleutian ? (That sturdy Tlingit.)
Mr. Big-Bang ? Or Alfred Anthopomorphic Autonomy ?
Who stoops to scoop mud
(To make or re-make eyes)
When stars belong to him !
When he counts and labels them like marbles !
"Blew breath?" Dust flung about by a hurricane !
Breathed into?
"What have spirit and matter to do with each other ?"

And I say, ask the windy mud-man, yourself :
What have thought and excrement in common --
Except you?

Land, Light, Wind and Water

Mud lies yet in our ditches,
In the swales and field lakes,
In the trails and cattle tracks,
The wheel ruts and prairie puddles :
Slippery plasma, stinking stuff,
Sticky to boot, on boots and tractor treads.
Mud without God's breath
Impedes the foot of walking mud.

The antique seas they say waved these wastes,
(Noah's natatorium?) left mud a-plenty
With fossil beasts of many sorts,
Like the prehistoric creatures
That crowd our pasture ponds in a wet year
Generated out of mud? By what breath ?

VI. Dust

A mote, a mite of emaciated mud
Dried up, broken up, sucked up by the wind,
Floats the free breeze on a determined journey
In proximity to, in suspension with myriad others --
But never quite meeting, merging --
Driven in the gale or floating in the sunbeam.

The labors of the farm-wife to remove it
From window-sills, from shelves and cupboards,
From every horizontal surface cannot succeed,
Not though she hound her husband (and he consent)

Land, Light, Wind and Water

To plant a lawn around the house,
To haul the road to a greater remove,
And leave his mud-boots at the door.

It is a mote of relatively no consequence
To the wind, its breath.
For the wind will go on when the dust grain settles
Or is washed down into the unified mud of rain.
On the windowsills of the universe it is clutter
But on microscope slide a universe itself.

The precious inch of topsoil
That makes and breaks the virgin prairie
Disappears as dust or its waterborne equivalent.
Dust colors the sky, blown miles into the atmosphere,
Gives beauty to the sunset as well as life
To flowering grass -- all three evanescent.

But when the clouds bend down,
The long fingers of heaven
Knead the baked up dirt :
Their gentle tips coax, enable,
Make a rising dough out of droughty dust.

VII. Prairie

Prairie is land without perspective,
With no mid-ground, no medium-sized object.
Like the sky it submits to, it is infinite or infinitesimal
With nothing of note in between.

Land, Light, Wind and Water

Undulating horizon or shrub and grass,
Prairie will not conform to the middle class.
Prairie is the pathway for pilgrims,
Alien fanatics not content, not satisfied: quasi-questors
Not willing to consent to conventional living
In a myth of permanence.

Prairie is an extremist's environment,
Equal parts of miracle and suffering ;
Desperation, insuperability,
Or grace, abundances of amazing provision.
Prairie is a land of few shadows, shadow-land
Of an imminent domain beneath the land,
Beyond the horizon :
A perspective that won't pass away.

Much of the prairie has been plowed up
In temporary elations and disappointments,
In destruction of minute microcosms
And briefly sacred ecosystems.
But the black-footed ferret is tougher than we think,
And eats far fewer of its young.

The prairie persists.
It may wave another buffalo grass good-bye
At its return and our departure.

VIII. Mirage

A mirage, I say, and you reel up
From the depths of the well of your imagination
A desert phantom, a sirenic spell,
Evil-cast to destroy the wanderer,
Crack his lips, his body, his mind.
Imagination, I say, and you try to lift
Your brow-wrinkled mind by its own bootstraps.
But you do not think of a place of images,
Multi-faceted faces of gems,

Here in this silt, this muck and mist,
Accumulations of cold desert nights
Blown about, grown about in dunes,
And baked like mirages at weak mind's noons.

But what is a mirage?
An image susceptible to the laws of physics,
Cast by no evil but the atmosphere
Into a place where its substance is not.

Then why do you damn your mind's mirages,
Dreams, ghosts, and secret hopes,
Or damn them doubly by claiming they're all,
Or all is they, wavering illusions?

A mirage, an image, an elusive thought --
These only exist as some sorts of traces
Of water, caravans, men, love,
Death, a creator, and heavenly places.

Land, Light, Wind and Water

IX. Agriculture

Agricola, agrico-lie, Latin for farmer and what he lives by :
Harvest and hail two distillations of the possible ends of his
    cultivations.
For the farmer, cynic though he seem, is a man of extensive
    faith,
Believing in blessing and cursing beyond all believing.

That's why he's so quick and so slow to buy the latest
    machine
Or method come down the pike.
That's why he's either very religious or very irreligious.
That's why his wife is a saint or a wreck.

He gets up in the morning and looks out the window
To make sure nobody has taken the farm, then he does the
    chores.
Then goes in for breakfast, as platonically idealized,
And heads from there straight into the labors of the day.

Although agriculture is the cultivation of the land
For the production of crops, the farmer doesn't think of it like
    that.
To him agriculture is a crap throw in a concentration camp,
A gamble within the bounds of insufferable servitude.

But any prison expands in time to become a universe,
A full scope for living, thus the farmer buys his daily number
In the stiffly stacked odds of his yearly lottery
Against weather and heat.

Soil is plowed, a field is planted, but the land is not farmed.
No more than the ocean is fished, or the sky hunted.

Land, Light, Wind and Water

Man can get no purchase on the land, no real grip on its skin.
And he has little more claim on what comes up than on his
    children.

But what the farmer does produce, the tosses he wins
Are worth more on this temporal scale of values
Than the so called technology and hot air the rest of us put
    out,
Which is only to say he is king over a very poor people.

Although man can denude fields, farms, even a whole
    countryside
For agricultural purposes -- when he's done, it's still the land.
That's no argument against crop rotation or strip farming and
    the like.
But it's fact, ma'am, no brag.

So the best a farmer can do with the land is massage it a little,
Like a flea on a bear -- and then bite gently.
Like the weatherman the farmer's a myth, a sometimes useful
    fiction.
He's our representative marking time against the thistles.

X. Rough Roads

    I am no longer surprised my children fall asleep
    As we drive rough gravel roads,
    Recalling other children gone
    Over unpaved roads to country farms

Where good companions, food, and talk
Made them loth to leave.
Loaded again by parental decree,
At last borne back over ruts and bumps,
Through smell of dust
To motor-hum, rock-rung frame and fenders,
We always fell asleep.
So my children on these rare mountain roads
Where the ride is roughest, slumber soundly.
It makes me wonder along which roads
Will we soonest find rest and better?

XI. Dirt Roads and Gravel

Dust will rise from either road,
Dirt or gravel, unpaved all.
Journeyor man, from the beginning,
Leaves paths, tracks, ruts and scars
Until passage enough makes a road.
In those rare places where prairie is still virgin,
Or when crops are just so, or from the air,
One may see old pathways yet --
Indian trails, or Grandfather's old wagon route
Across the hills and down for water --
But most of the trails are now roads,
And most of the roads now graveled.
Dirt roads, smooth, soft tracks seem better
In all seasons of clemency,
Early, easy ways of mercy.

But when hard rains come,
Gravel roads are best,
Though they are uncomfortable,
Harsh, loud, rough, in good weather.
And see, it is from the gravel roads
The most dust arises.

XII. The High Places

Not only Ararat, but Sinai, also, of Israel's great mountains
Was not in Israel at all --
Remember the greatest of God's promises
May come to us beyond beloved borders.

But Israel's mountains were important, so ours.
Their Bethel, Carmel, Ebal and Gerizim,
Gilead, Hermon, Horeb and Olivet,
Peor, Seir, Tabor and Zion.
And our Highwood Baldy with attendant peaks,
The distant Bear Paws, the Little Belts,
Square Butte, and on a clear day
'Way up in Canada, the Sweetgrass Hills.
Landmarks all, points to navigate by,
Casting their shadows and names around them.

Israel made covenants, gave pledges on its mountains.
From time to time so do we.
Standing on a mountain one has a clearer sense of eternity,
Of distance and perspective, and magnificence.

Land, Light, Wind and Water

Perhaps that's why the little shrines,
The Baal temples and altars sprang up again and again
On Israel's high places.
Ever since Lewis and Clark, the Jedidiah Smiths among us
Have conquered and been conquered by the high places,
Been lured on and down as we have gone up the mountains
To know, to see, to stand over the creation,
And -- just a little twist -- to rule there.

Why does the wilderness belong to the demons ?
To whom did the Baal-worshippers sacrifice their children ?
Why appropriate the pleasant groves on top of the hills ?

God's mercy has made our mountain tops uninhabitable.
They are terrible in winter -- hells of wind and ice.
So we live on the plains, and only lift our eyes to the hills
To ask, what help is there? Where will it come from ?
But sometimes we climb them, and briefly lose the answer,
Tempted to worship we know not quite what,
In order to rule the universe.
What mercy that Golgotha is a hill,
For none of these mountains will fall on us at need.

It was on Carmel that Elijah challenged God,
Moses longed from Pisgah, but could not pass over.

XIII. The Buffalo Jump

    At the Museum of the Plains Indian,
    In panoramic pathos is portrayed

The buffalo jump, Blackfoot *piskun*
The massed destructive descent
Of behemoth bison, powerful, powerless
In acts of losing their footings,
Surrendering amidst the goading
Of their fellows to the pretty wiles
Of the practiced ancient native ;
Falling furious, fear-shot, lost,
Headlong, horned heads their own hooking,
Down, out of dignity, to death: detritus.
It is difficult not to mourn
A creature, a way of life, a time,
And people gone forever ;
Gone like the suicidal poets
Who briefly graced our uneven soils
Before a slinking Judas angel
Led them to their buffaloed jumps :
Beloved heroic herd,
Which might have fed an age of wanderers,
Now bones and shattered verse.

XIV. *Gather Stones Together*

Stones gathered, landmarks of fields,
Seried mounds against straight fencerows,
Monuments, those piles at corners,
Rounded stone, cracked boulders, glacial baggage,
Were bitter burdens for the first farmers.

Land, Light, Wind and Water

I was privileged to hearken back
One time my cousin broke government land,
Virgin plain, thitherto unturned,
Where I was set to gathering stones.
Snuffing broken earth perfume,
I embraced the work, a young man's revel,
Back and shoulders, fingers and wrists :
The bigger the boulder, the better
For a head-strong, heart-strong boy.

But there were stones a-plenty left
For homesteaders old, worn, and broken.
The still stone stacks around our fields
Were piled by Jenny as well as John,
Nor was she a brawny woman.
Yet rocks remain in the midst of fields
Where many back-bent years they gathered.

I'd yet to feel and know the strain,
New and briefly gathering stones
From the turned black, almost friendly earth
Before the season of scattering.

XV. This Is a Desert Place

" This is a desert place and now the time is far passed."
That is the moan of our malaise, those words, that fact.
A dimly lit burnt over waste
It might as well be Death Valley at dusk.

Land, Light, Wind and Water

And although there is no hope
We can at least cut our losses,
Act with some dignity
In our everlasting hunger.
We can at least go somewhere
Out of each other's sight to be miserable.

Don't string me out, string us out,
String them out any further, Lord.
Send us away !

Desert, Lord, just as the early explorers labeled it,
The time is all passed :
What was of abundance, what was of opportunity --
Gone.

Please don't confuse the issue with little exceptions !
Send away the kid with his cheerful face, his loaves and
       fishes.
We're talking about drought and dearth :
The Great American Desert! Saharas! Gobis! . . . desolation !
And clocks striking deep at empty midnight.

Yesterday? Yes, I ate . . . but it is passed,
As are the ancient days of plenty
And today there is not enough . . .

Baskets of fragments ?

XVI. Promised Land

Some say it's just a harkening back to Eden,
This longing, this inner certainty about a promised land.
Lord knows we encounter plenty of flaming swords
In our attempts to return.

Others say it's just a reaction to being cheated in Egypt,
To being sold a boomer's lie about plenty and freedom in
      Gilead--
A tale that turned into a dirge as our flocks were taken,
And we bend our backs gathering straw for someone else's
      bricks,
Someone else's monuments to someone else's power.

Some say the long wandering made our footloose fancies
Permanently footsore. Tired of wilderness dependency
We've become fixated on a place to own
Flowing with milk and honey and rest.

All of the above and more makes us believe it,
Makes us willing to drive heathen from our hearts,
And still be weary foot soldiers taking the cities,
Taking the countryside we've been led to.

Not just for the land's sake, but also for the promise.

> *And I'm bound for the promised land ...*
> *Oh, I'm bound for the promised land ...*
> *Who will come and go with me ?*
> *I'm bound for the promised land.*

This land will not sustain us. " Landsake, it's a pity, "
But the Story starts in a garden and ends in a city.

Land, Light, Wind and Water

Land, Light, Wind and Water

THE BIG LIGHTS

The poets light but lamps, Themselves go out.
    -- Emily Dickinson

The Big Lights

God said let there be light
Back when heavenly-minded talk had more sway,
And the lights were, greater and lesser,
By day and night when there were no other firmaments.

But men are not content with mere diminution,
Clamor always for a lot less.
It is the hand-wicked pin-prick lights
About which society turns.
Turns ever without reference to the heavens
Or words issuing therefrom.

Outcasts, nomadic families
Spotting the dark void of plains with glimmers
Away from the rotting glow of cities,
Find least lights less fascinating.

Land, Light, Wind and Water

The big lights light what needs lightening ;
While lights of homesteads, farms and homes
Have come and gone, they lingered.

The big lights are pilgrims
Like dwellers on plains and mountains :
Wander through the year, periodically settle down ;
Haphazard strangers and aliens,
Having here no continuing city, but perhaps seeking.

And if the shekinah glory that blinded Isaiah and Saul
No longer shines in Israel's aether,
Still we seek some glimpse of God's back
In what comes across our sky --
Wait for the light in his cloud-breaking front.

Meanwhile we experience few miracles as most count
    them :
St. Elmo's fire dancing on the cattle's horns
Or tips of telephone poles, is rare, now --
Although some see it -- more than know St. Elmo.
At worst of winter, sun dogs mimic the besieged orb.
And once in a blue moon, the sun is blotted from the sky.
Or sometimes the world shades away the moon.
Stray comets, surprising all, may light the night,
And it is said when the sun is low
One may see a halo about his shadow
In the low-cropped stubble or a gravel bed,
As utility poles cast shadows, cross the land.

But the big lights, those first created things,
Circuit preachers, frontier Jesuits,
Carry exodus and return
Across the deserts of our days ;

Land, Light, Wind and Water

Variations on the same gospel
Every time they pass.
They preach in tents, in barnyards,
And through the shaded tavern windows.
They flare through the night
In which their minder needs nor nods.

I. Dawn Light

The dawn light is no bringer of hope :
Dark hid so much best hidden.
Rosy-fingered said blind Homer --
Ham-handed say the farmboys, men, women.

Sleep, that thousand deaths we die
Before the last, is not cowardly ;
Shades and protects, feeds us,
Offers opiate oblivion, dissolves
Our dealings with hope or despair.
But dawn comes pale pink like a chorus girl
Bringing nothing but trouble.
All the burdens which night led away
Lumber back, loom up before us,
Murmur to men who curse them you are cursed.

On the reservoir the far fliers,
The wide-V'd voyageurs are first to smell it ;
Out upon the broad sea of their summering,
And hail one another at the first crack.
(Red sky at morning, sailors take warning.)
The muskrats punt to and fro,

Blackbirds shoulder their beacons
On the towers of cattail
All along the shoaly coast.
Water creatures count the toll of stormy night :
Around the bruised reed ravished banks
Flurries of fur and feathers
Testify to ravages the dark hid.

Yet some days dawned exceptional :
High upon the mountain, there -- Baldy --
Two cousins, brother and I awoke
One morning in teeth-chattering celebration
Of the dawn-day of my majority.
Yes, Homer, dawn was rosy-fingered then.
We watched it creep across the ridges
Of plain and mountains,
Leaving coulees and canyons in masked indigo.
As light leapt to that high peak
Where I huddled jubilant on a rock ;
It focused first on a clump of harebells,
Purple still with close-knit night.
Up buoyed the inexorable orb, exploded,
Hurling un-atomic rays through dim drops,
Dew hung on every needle-stunted pine,
Each brief-bowed blade of alpine grass,
Training rainbows everywhere.

Yet, mornings, immediate,
Dirty old dawn comes clumping in
And catches us out of bed
By the corners of our eyes.

II. Morning Light

Day has come *de facto*
While in the early morning light
The phenomenon beginning lingers.
A thin dew covers the native grass
Where cottontails graze in long shadows
As though there were no such things as cynics.
A time for chores, bacon-boasting breakfast,
Machinery and animal noises, odors,
Feeding, oiling, getting ready.
We are about the tasks appointed us,
After blinking sleep dead.
Now we recognize how much needs doing,
But believe much may be done ;
Trust in ours and others' powers to do,
Look forward to what shall be accomplished.
Hope seeps shallow out of the broad land
In the oblique rays of morning.

III. Midsummer Sun

Midday at midsummer
Shows all vanity beneath the sun.
Long and dreary are those days,
Those hours of sending back
The desperate beat of our temples
Against the unrelenting pulsing light.

Land, Light, Wind and Water

There is nothing new, all is old,
Growing interminably older.
The wax wanes in each brief candle.
We must work hardest
When the sunlight is most unmerciful ;
Our labors are desperate :
Plowing the summer fallow, fighting sun-sprung weeds ;
Cutting and threshing sun-parched grain,
Hurrying it to the granaries
Before the sun-spurred wind whips and shatters it,
Or brings the thirsty thunder storm.
We have no strength to wonder
At butterflies in frantic aimlessness,
Fleeing terrible sapphire skies.
Shimmering witchwater springs on roads, lakebeds ;
Mirages waver over visions, plains,
As fevered heads concoct hot images
For eyes of sense and faith to barely blink away.
Under incandescent Canadian crystal
We long, gaze from our heated machines,
On diminishing reservoirs, dazed streams,
Dreaming of beer, lemonade, water,
But a drop to cool our tongues.
We find some brief relief divvying
Dusted canvas contents of the water bag
Which cools best when the sun turns fiercest,
Fiery noon whirling in the wheel of summer.

IV. Summer Clouds

In Platonic blue skies
Clouds are embodiments of light,
Coming unexpected with radiance.
Those who describe them in cotton terms
Must meditate on piteous clouds ;
Likewise likeners to sheep --
Can they know flocks or weather ?
These white phenomena frequenting
The distilled skies of summer's spring
Are not nursery rhyme illustrations,
Small, innocent sky-dabs ;
But accumulated nimbuses of saints
Haloeing earth in unearthly purity.
Less mist than mystery,
They tower up, looming down
Upon us like Wordsworth's mountain,
Inspiring the same awe.
But these also bring comfort,
Blessed shade descending
(Risen from dead, entombed waters)
Is blessed shelter from unrelieved light.
They move magnificent, destined.
Perhaps they will bleed rain on us unjust,
Before we're left impoverished of their presence.
Yet sometimes, when they are no bigger
Than a man's hand,
One may look a little like the whitest lamb
If lambs were made of light.

V. *The Light of Fall*

The light of fall is a will-'o-the-wisp,
Driven, harried, windblown gray.
(Who has seen the wind? Neither you nor I
But when the light bows down its head . . .)
The light of fall is John light :
Baptist, presaging an awesome advent ;
Revelator, harbinging apocalypse --
A thin light between life and death,
Life-light and death-light traced dimly
In the two angles of high-flying geese.
It is a driven light, submitting to the wind,
Delivering itself up to the air's buffeting
Without complaint, without comfort of sun or sky
Now hidden, hallowed by the sickly, torn vapors
Enshrouding our wide land,
Never so flat as in the fall.
The windblown light of fall
Hurries from and hurries to,
But carries no expectation of escape or sanctuary,
Offers no hope, withholds all grounds
For despair : shouldering only uneasiness.
The light fades and intensifies
With the flow of clouds,
The lesser and greater density of obfuscation,
Until at last the overcast light of fall
Is entirely blown away
With the coming of sighing night.

Land, Light, Wind and Water

VI. The Light of Falling Snow

In the light of falling snow
One wants no other light,
No other time or other fall,
Otherworldly as lightless night.
Light falls, soft, blue-kissed,
In lumps, great particles, theory no longer.
Men and children stand entranced at windows,
Or hurry home to stomp and stand.
Those first here -- long, lean peoples --
Walked or rode their weary miles,
With savvy and some wisdom ;
Yet the mesmerizing blizzards
Dazed some of them as they daze us :
The too much light put out their own.
Slipping into dragging drifts,
Some dropped to sleep, no shelter,
Never threw off the comfortable blanket.
Safe-havened, we are flattered to feel
The close familiarity,
The falling light, angelic white ;
Are almost fooled despite knowing
This light is more than match for men,
Deceiving most often the strong.

VII. Clear Day After Snow

After snow has come down
There is no more night.

Stars' light, alone, illumines all,
Reflected over the great expanse
In their miniscule fallen images.
Nor is there dawn,
But only brilliance onward
From the sun's first messenger.
Laughing at our blindness,
We stumble out of doors,
Unaccustomed to our newly-clothed largeness.
The sun is all light now,
Once so much heat to us,
And we are thankful --
For the turned-chapped cheeks, the numb hands,
The much alive sensation.
Illumined by the fallen snow.
All tracks are clear, blue dashes ;
Map every creature, mouse and bird ;
Record each struggle, each escape,
Each capture, death or turning aside.
Few things stay hidden or doubtful.
Now we travel at large and do not tire ;
Go our second mile
Safe in the revelation of radiance,
In the new world white
Under bluest sides.

The mountains catch the light first
And give it up latest.
Our rain is their sleet,
Our sleet, their snow --
Reminding us of purity
Before we have our own.

Land, Light, Wind and Water

VIII. Spring Light

Though winter wore but two moods
And changed her clothes accordingly,
Brilliant white or drab brown, bride or scrubwoman,
Spring is all subtlety.
The light of spring is doled out
By a dazed sun to a long-suffered world :
Conspirators who conceive
Small beginnings, early tests
To put to proof the revolution.
Then upon an unlikely hill,
Where the sun has weakly watered the dry
And matted grasses with hoarded light,
A firstfruit springs and offers itself
In bolder gold than the light has dared.
A fritillary nods, head-bowed humble,
Others join the yellowbell -- next, and next.
In these the light of spring first shines,
Emboldens itself by objective fact
Of its power to remake, renew earth,
Begun in so tiny a flower.
Thence it surges in heartier waves,
Light soon heat, through grasses first shoots,
Streams, new ringers, returning new singers :
Red-winged blackbirds, meadowlarks,
With voices full of flowing light.
Suddenly flourishing full of force,
Earth bustles forth, new confident --
Parades all their progeny before
The beaming sun of spring.

Land, Light, Wind and Water

IX. *Storm Light*

The gray stampede, driving awe before it,
Rose up out of a distant rumor,
Skirting the mountains by southwest
And came relentless --
As buffalo herds must have come.
The small devastation of rain somewhat
Relieved the fierce unknowing in the wind.
The deadly light that flickered far off
Suddenly flashed fanatic around us :
White light flung back the few shadows,
The little hiding the storm left us --
The crack and long roll rang inevitable
Words to truth.
Few hearts were lightened,
Although a Viking few exalted themselves --
In wistful hubris -- imagining their pyres.
And the storm passed.
Seldom, so seldom was any struck
By that brilliant, pure power,
(Although most were shaken by the reports).
The dissolving line seemed hardly significant
As it rolled northeast and over the horizon.
Our deep-set awe at the light of storm faded,
Forgotten as we sat to supper.

X. Light Before Hail

Hail light is rare enough one nearly forgets,
Until it shines again
From storm clouds sick with a terrible malady,
Green hued and green-lighting all.
Our stomachs turned sick, too,
Caught the plague of their contagion,
As the wind sank for a heart-beating moment
In the subterranean atmosphere
Before the sky hurled ice.
Corna caldast, the coldest grain,
Harvesting all other without mercy :
Like Leviathan, without bridle or bit ;
Reaping where another had sown in tears.
Arbitrarily cutting mile-wide swaths,
It might follow fencerows, never cross the wire.
As it struck, its light was quickly forgotten
By minds misted over miles of destruction
Under cloud-tossed spheres, the frozen frenzy
Of freak weather leaped from heaven to fields.

Among the lights hail light was rare,
Nevertheless it harries my dreams
Like a Spanish painting: it cannot be right,
Not the color; not the boding ;
Not the smell.

XI. Two Sides of the Sky

The storms come so briefly, but so suddenly
In the midst of summer,
That stormlight and a bright day
Often show in the same high ceiling.
I have them both fixed in my mind's eye,
Can see the battle-line between them
Shift across the sky :
The overwhelming light of mid-day
Swept before the ordered front of darkness
Into despondent light of storm ;
The squall and the dust; the dread of destruction
In an unpredictable flick of built-up justice
Here or there in a chaotic world.
But stormlight, and lightning, too, give back
Before the clean, wet winds,
Which flap their aprons at last and shoo
The mumbling mob out the sky's gate ;
So that one day, clear -- clear as vision
In my mirror-dark, often cloudy memory,
We stood in the back door and watched the storm rage,
Cast hastily spoken rain over all ;
Then went to the front door and looked out
On the bouyant light of forgiving evening,
Which wouldn't have lifted our hearts so --
Were we not so fresh from the other.

XII. Lightning

God, say the Madison Avenue mystics, the money changers,
The Eastern magi following their own stars,
God, is whoever you want him to be.
VUK-AVOOM! says the thunder, but the lightning flashed
    first.
Evil, say the snake-tongue-oil peddlers, the bait and switch
    artists,
The soul-sold spirit sellers in their getaway wagons,
Evil is a state of mind, a temporary phenomenon.
TCH-TCH-KUR-ACK! says the lightning before the thunder
    breathed.
If there were no charges in the clouds
And none on earth, there would be no lightning.
If the mass of electrons
Did not sweep across plains to a lone pole,
The lone tree -- or man, there would be no destruction,
No split, no cinders, no body to bury ;
No arcing leap from earth to heaven
And perhaps no sweet rain.

The few who do homage at God's tomb
Meet figures dressed in lightning.

XIII. Rainbow Light

After the storm, the worse the better
Were rainbows springing in the south :
Spectacles of fractured light,
Broken for us through cosmic bending,
Sunlight simplified in more complex form
Through unethereal earth's atmosphere.
Rainbows, sublimations in our sight
Were vaults against the mountains,
Over well-watered fields, vistas of green,
Or venerable ready harvests.
Can one's mind possibly have refined
Them purer than they were ?
No, photographs, paintings testify
To a rarity mind nor emulsion could capture.
There were always two, if there was one ;
One higher, less lucid -- translucent
To the point of being imperceptible in the periphery ;
The other brilliant with colors substantial,
Promising an earth-free treasure.
The only unity we confess -- the sky --
Was broken in two, not segments only
But two shades by the brighter arc,
Separating all to its left and right,
As we gazed across the rain-fresh land
Puzzled in light of promise.

XIV. Firelight

Ofttimes briefly among the big lights
Fires flare up from Promethean efforts,
Singe our memories, leave scars and red fears.
Fires, making their presences known
In challenges, white, black and gray
Sent toward heaven, were often man-lit.

(Although sometimes a lightning smoke
Hung in the south over summer mountains.)
It was trains, trucks, wet grain, wiring
Lit our fires -- man's heart-fired labors, dark-driving desire
To overcome weather, limitation.
Who lights his own torch throws sparks all around.

Field fires kindled an awful thrill,
Offered chances for heroism, perhaps --
Like Dad rushing out
To plow a strip around a neighbor's quick-harvest fire --
But never profitable except in terror.
Homes, elevators, oil tanks, right-of-ways :
We saw all and will not forget.
The big lights are clearer, if not safer,
Even darkness brighter than most man-fires.

But little fires, candles, camp rock rings,
Lanterns, properly trimmed and kept,
Are lights within man's lowly province,
Lovely in humble places.

XV. Evening Light

Evening comes with evanescent light
And we rejoice, despite its brevity,
In the thorough sense of having done :
The fatalist grasp we can sail no further
In the calm that flows across the land,
The oblique light of evening.

Things stand out themselves,
Shadows far-reaching, hues truer and fresh,
Now we're about to lose them.
Nighthawks man the crow's-nest of sky
In the late minutes of unearthly calm :
Stoop and winnow un-voiced cries,
Feather-plumbed soundings of sinking sun.

In the eternal calm of this brief bay
Between end of labor and end of waking,
We found much joy, exhilaration --
Playing desperately at tag or toss,
Father, brothers, sister, dog,
Across the broad yard and into the swale,
Before going in to supper.
On the reservoir reflections
Of gathering ducks at dimming dusk
Were undisturbed by our frenzy of peace.
When those moments ended, evening light died,
In climax of sunset,
Or fading mist of subtle night.

During harvest, just before, just after,
The evening dusk grew bolder :

Land, Light, Wind and Water

Lingered, declaring day dominated night,

And took to levying taxes.
The land, the labor under its sway,
Were each assessed their mite of motes.
The processions of those paying these tributes
Crossed the land in solemn approaches,
Small, and respectful against the expanse.
Plowers sent up silver dust ;
Drivers tendered tolls of the same ;
The harvesters offered gold,

Which hung, ready for counting,
Along the roads, in hollows of fields,
As evening light tallied the last.
Reverently engines sang like monks
Returning home from the dusky fields.

XVI. *Sunset*

Everyday the sun sets -- so far, at least --
But sometimes merely in a setting of sun ;
Other times, in a sun-set.
If there are no clouds, the sun goes down
Before your eyes :
The disc you thought insuperable,
The radiance you could not bear,
Begins to fade two feet above the black horizon :

Land, Light, Wind and Water

Turning visible, yellow, then fierce orange,
Then red, one foot only out of the grave
And settles down, perceptibly ;
Scarcely perching on the edge of sky,
Nor lingering to rest.
Reminding of former incandescence,
It seems to burn into the land
Its diameter's depth, like a welder's arc ;
Dims violently, and sinks like a stone,
Leaving a smudge of dirty orange
Floating wrack on the rim of sky.

But when there are clouds,
There may be spectacles
In proportion to the body
Of those neutralized lights
And the day's temperament.
Sunset may still be a shoddy affair,
Pale penurious ennui,
Like the last act of a one ring circus
Which has traveled too far,
Eaten too much dust.
Then, the clouds indistinct, the colors pale,
The effects disappoint young farm children,
Sick to their stomachs on cotton candy.

But the sunsets which are in all our minds
When we speak that word of quiet power
Are too glorious for me or you
To describe in truth or poetry.
These come unpredictably, startling shows
Exuberant, extravagant with wonders ;
Seldom many nights in one place -- passing dreams.
Sometimes after an early storm

Land, Light, Wind and Water

Clouds deploy in feudal phalanxes ;
Figures of finery; fugues of dance ;
While the sun blows
Blasted by some bellows and glows
Molten golden and flows beneath
The lowermost ranks along the floor.
But the radiance of phenomenal fire
Lights higher clouds orange, red, and crimson,
Tinges every tint-tossed tier
Lines from below in succeeding shades
Until indigo evening inundates,
Involves, envelops, drowns the rays
Broke from below
Like arc-lights in storm,
Defenders' last stand in the teeth of night,
Which certain to win,
Makes hues denser, music more intense,
As it presses down.
The gold goes out; orange, purple ranks
Retreat across the field of sky,
Falling down into darkness.

We linger after the glory fades,
Hoping one night it will stay forever.

XVII. Twilight

Our twilight, two-light, 'tween-light,
Was no Ragnarok of gods,

No agony of heaven,
But night born painlessly
Out of a sleep-slid sky.
Sunset over, starlight flickering into being
Against ghostly gloaming, always
Least substantial of earthly shines --
Perhaps, most substantial in the other world.
White-light gone into long memory,
But pale red whispers beyond the hills
Echo faintly Hosanna -- Crucify --
And He is Risen.

The crack between heaven and earth
Revealed for so few moments
Closes down again
And leaves us alone with our exhaustion,
Our own twilit sleep
In which to bear brief burdens, candles
For yet a few groans of creation.

XVIII. Reflections

The best seeing is not always bare,
Direct vision of many things may blind --
The welder's arc, the sun's orb, God's face.
I watched my only eclipse of sun
In the shadows of locust-chewed leaves
Beneath a sun-plagued tree
A reflection from the ground
Through dim means of my insect lenses.

I saw it clearly ;
And used to look at moon and stars
Through reflecting scope, a birthday gift.
Every image we believe we perceive
(Except of lights, the lights, themselves)
We take in, photograph by reflection.
Crazy mirrors at county fairs or moonshine
Remind us to temper trust,
But we live and build on fruits of reflection.
The finest nuances are there, too,
Beauty and mood and recollection
Reflected in rivers, reservoirs, lakes, --
Long, wavering sun-paths, skipping moon faces,
Or quavering star-spots ;
Shattered and scattered and far-spread,
Silhouetting loved ones or places,
Which shimmer through memory in reflected light.

XIX. Moonlight

The influences of the moon
Need no other ocean
Than the horizon of prairie
Or human hearts.
The moon's light waxes
And night neaps on the Edison-abandoned plains.
The pale light the moon sends on
Seems great gift,
Unless one consider what it keeps back.

Its thin beams appear more than are :
An illusion, luring us to lunacy,
The moon's dark side.
Once, coming home in my father's truck,
I turned off headlights
Plunging along a near-radiant road,
Silver dust of moon-beaming earth
Lit by the moon's manic gold,
And careened into a ditch --

Certain of the track: certain wrong.
Moonstruck lovers fantastic
With illumination the satellite
(No light of its own) barely gives,
Sicken after a time
Of exhaustion, of emotional exertion :
Are pulled with the tides into worse undertows
Beneath moons quarter, full, or half

Yet the moon looms large,
Seems to outshine its source
As long as the latter lends it light,
And remains hidden.

XX. Starlight

The Blackfoots have a tale of bear
Explaining the Big Dipper in Ursa Major,
But not how Greeks, Romans, and Germans

Land, Light, Wind and Water

Came to see a bear there, too.
The dark-enshrouded tale of starlight
Has focused more than worldwide eyes,
Brought mankind to meditate
On more than sky-borne creatures.
Why is starlight liquid, clear,
Or associated with music and truth ?
Yet of the sum of mankind's hours,
Few are spent watching still stars --

We prefer not to ponder.
Our astronomical time is given
More to looking for heavenly *doings*,
Than for any astral vision of being :
We counted falling stars, meteorites
In the warm grass nights of midsummer's length.
As many as ten star-streaks per minute
We saw and counted without much awe.
Sometimes scientific we split the sky,
Sitting back to back smugly all-seeing,
Taking the tally of sky-slipped travelers.
Some of those lights fell, streaked half heaven,
Filling us with a kind of delight.
We learned the North Star and a few constellations.

The Blackfoots kept sidereal time
By the "Little Brother" in the Big Dipper :
The stars have practical uses to land
As well as to ocean voyagers,
But few can look for long at the stars.
They don't blind eyes like unseeable sun,
But throw over minds a cloud of unknowing,
Make men worry and wonder.

Only on clear nights with snow-covered ground
Does starlight illuminate much.
Yet men the world over, from corners of eyes,
Look at the stars and think the same thoughts,
How far, how many, who made them? Why.

XXI. The Northern Lights

Sometimes our day ended as it began,
With northern lights -- Aurora borealis,
Originally the "northern dawn".
Yet one dawn is disparate from the other
In more than the day's dial's measure.
While dawn awakened us to brief hopes,
Northern lights are benedictions
Glowing in the low north,
Usually in late summer, sometimes barely an aura.
But other times they are more,
Blessing our vision beyond seeing.
Once on an evening already memorable,
We rode back from late-loved mountains,
Friends and cousins, all worn out ;
Until we stopped, to watch, to gaze,
To wonder in awe at the unveiled sky :
A pageant unfolding in the distant north,
Pale yellow, then red, into green and blue,
Long curtains of light parting and joining,
Rippling across the horizon in folds

Land, Light, Wind and Water

As clearly defined as those of a theatre,
But never static in form or field.
The forms of canyons and chasms grew greater
Until they seemed to have crossed the plateau
Where most of our homes and farms lay dark.
We prayed aloud with our eyes open,
Thanked God in ecstatic seeing,
Our hearts' grasping, and asked again
Of Aurora's maker Tithonus' boon, without his error.

The lights grew dimmer, receded again;
We drove on north where the last color flickered,
The last light curtain closed.

XXII. *Conclusion*

The lights faded, every one.
The lights of yesterday, of Montana,
Of last night, are far from us now.
Soon I will be far --
Faded and far from those I love,
Those I have not met to love
Or spoken to -- not a word.
Night with its rubbing dreams
Is too little reason to fear or hope.

It is only the light beyond the lights
That makes them big, that brightens deep,
Moves heart to joy beyond the world.

Land, Light, Wind and Water

As I was an exile beyond the River,
Among captive aliens,
God's forgetting people,
I saw the lights, and was struck, awed.
Watching wheels of refulgence make straight paths
Across the sky to the white cloud throne
Beneath the terrible crystal.
The light of rainbows, sun, moon and stars
Came out from one in the form of a man
Bright in a flash of lightning.

All creatures: eagle, bull, lion, and men
Were in the midst of the lights,
By them ordered their coming and going.
A voice in the lights spoke to me saying,
Son of man stand on your feet.
Dimly in his light I do.

Land, Light, Wind and Water

WHAT THE WIND SAID

The wind bloweth where it listeth, and thou hearest the sound thereof, but canst not tell whence it cometh, and whither it goeth: so is every one that is born of the Spirit.
-- The Gospel of John, 3:8

I. Unseen Forces

The wind is ash, fuel, fire --
Consuming all along its edge.
The wind is sailor, sea and seine
Steadily thrown, never brought up empty.
It scatters, covers, harvests and winnows,
Drives seed up, over, and shatters
Brave beginnings and onerous endings
Before the onslaught that hardly ceases.

There are shelterbelts.
There are buildings . . .
Houses, sheds, towers, barns,
There are sweaters, coats, scarves and caps.
But I have seen a hat sail like a headstrong bird
A hundred yards and land running.
Yes, and I have seen a shed grown young,
Hop, skip and leap a reservoir
Before the livening force of storm.

Land, Light, Wind and Water

The Japanese compare bamboo and oaks
Before an unrelenting wind,
And bow to the bamboo,
But we have neither in these high prairies,
Only the seas of grass, wheat and barley,
Foam-cresting and rip-tidy with wind
Throughout most the year.

The wind blows where it will
Brings all we get: want, weal and weather.
So when I first heard that nursery rhyme,
A distant sigh from a frail lady,
It struck me as gospel :
" Who has seen the wind . . . ? "

II. Weathervane

There are not many weathervanes left.
I remember a few mounted atop barns or sheds
Pointing out where the wind blew --
Maybe it's because
The smallest boy or cat knew
Which way the wind was blowing
Without heeding how the weathercock sat.
Or maybe there weren't many weathervanes
Because the headstrong wind was so intent on tumbling
Those icons of wood or tin from their high places
To the humility of earth,
Making constant bother and repair

The rule for those who wished to gauge
The tides of the ocean of air.

There were three common shapes :
Crowing cock, running horse, and simple arrow,
Creaking to point the wind's course as tropes
Or types of something :
A thought or feeling --
Annunciation, hastening on,
Or an everlasting shot.

I remember one rusty rooster, half-cocked,
Already beginning to succumb to the relentless leverage
Of wind. Nevertheless (though out of plumb) it stood
On the highest barn around
Remote and high; was known
To all. Though most entertained doubt,
It caught us by the corner of the eye,
But we were hypocrites knowing how to read indicators
Of wind and weather, while not caring for other signs,
Though the rooster turn and squeak three times.

III. Winter Wind

Who has not walked out on a winter's night
(When it seems storms have beginning nor end)
Into the mauling arms of a gale
And madly taken two-steps further,
Ready to walk, run, stumble on

Land, Light, Wind and Water

Into the wild and soul-sweeping darkness
Without ever looking back ?

The Wendigo my father spoke of
('The WEN-N-N-d'go', with widening eyes)
Was far too real for a mere tale.
Everyone knows it though not all its name :
The soul-sucking wind warden,
Calling all to throw caution to the wind,
Oblivion's oblate, loughing lurer toward
The whirlpool world of will-less-ness.
Indeed, who would want to see the wind !

Outdoors, of course, we feel it.
Once, I remember, once only,
When our car stuck half a mile from the farm,
And we were alone, wife, baby and I,

I felt the full fear of what it might mean
To freeze in that wind, to die of cold.
How it bit me, as I struggled on foot
And, God's grace, got the tractor to run.

They were still warm -- unlike the neighbors
Of grandfather's lore who froze fifty feet
From their own front door.
Winter winds are the true irresistible foursome.

And even indoors, who hasn't heard
The sough, the scream, the brief susurrus,
Before it blasts and cries again
Around the corners and under the eaves.

Aye, winter wind, as bitter as any could wish.
But don't it sing to you !

Don't a man long for the feel of it in his face,
And hear a call from some windy place ?

IV. Wind Chill Factor

The breeze passing over the garden shriveled no vine.
It caressed naked flesh, a freshet on the face of the waters,
But the garden withered, something crept in, a worm in the
    root,
Or some chilly factor of climatic change. So now we worry,
Worry and listen carefully to the air-borne voices which
    predict
And compare with knowledge of good and evil.
There is more to it than cold and heat, more than mere
    weather
To be taken into consideration as we orient our pilgrimage.
The prairie and the mountains do not register it.
The grass, herbs, and the few gaunt broad-leafed trees
Are nakeder since the change, but need no cover.
Personification is not the danger but de-personification.
It is our particular flesh needs covering, protecting. We listen
To the acute calculations of wind chill factor.
Lichen-covered rocks have accepted the humiliation without
    blame,
They live for hundreds, perhaps millennial years
From forty below zero to a hundred-and-ten degrees.

With only a bicentennial crack or chip, the lichens
Tight in symbiosis, grow on, in ever-widening patches.

Life as we know it, the life of clean animals and ourselves,
Is threatened by the cold in the wind, the cold that makes
The wind much colder, fretting, freezing down to the heart.
The hills and cottonwoods stand stoically against attacks
Or yawns of wind. We cringe at any movement
While the mercury messages anything near freezing.
And since the question of ice or fire is not moot,
Will there be another factor to the last hot breeze ?

V. Chinook

Chinooks are somewhat peculiar to our locale,
But if you've known a haven of rest,
A time of joy in the midst of trouble,
You know about chinooks.
A warm wind brings balmy days
Along the mountains and melts the snow.
It fools the bees out of their hives,
And us out of our parkas.
"Snoweater" and "Black wind" the Blackfoots called it,
Black with a richness of warmth and hope ?
Charley Russell, the cowboy artist,
Mortalized it in paint --
One rib-racked steer in a field of snow.
"The Last of Five Thousand or Waiting for a Chinook".

Land, Light, Wind and Water

That's the trouble with promises,
They bear with them expectations,
And sometimes presumptions.

A chinook wind does not feel warm,
Snoweater that it is -- because it's so strong.
Nor does it sound a cheerful note, --
Mourning around our windows :
A wild horse neighing,
A lone wolf baying,
Young mother groaning,
An old man moaning.
It's what it does makes it so welcome,
Resurrecting spring in the midst of winter,
And giving us hints of surcease of sorrow.

VI. After the Chinook

You'd better bundle up.

VII. I'm Gonna Die

I'm gonna die, oh, I'm gonna die:
I don't know when, but I do know why,
I'm gonna die, oh, I'm gonna die:
I don't know when, but I do know why,
'Cause the streams all freeze and the birds all fly,
And the cold wind blows -- as the pine trees sigh.

Land, Light, Wind and Water

There's many a way that the cold wind blows.
There's many a thing that a man never knows,
But the wind shakes every standing tree
As the living truth is shaking me.

The seed must die so a tree can be born.
The sun must set to rise at morn;
And so we die but what's our end --
Does morning wait for us my friend?

The pine trees bend in the winter wind
And the wet snow breaks their weary limbs,
But when all else is dead and gone
These evergreens live on and on.

The maker planned and the maker made,
The moon don't blink and the stars don't fade,
So why when all was said and done
Did Adam fail? Why dimmed the sun?

The wind knows why he died on a tree;
The streams know why his blood flowed free;
The birds know why there were thorns on his head;
His children know why he rose from the dead.

The streams all melt and the birds return.
The spring wind blows through a waving fern;
It flows like a love that never ends;
It sings to us as though to friends.

I'm gonna die, oh, I'm gonna die:
I don't know when, but I do know why,
I'm gonna die, oh, I'm gonna die:
I don't know when, but I do know why,

'Cause the streams all freeze and the birds all fly,
And the cold wind blows -- as the pine trees sigh.

VIII. Spring Wind

To talk accurately about spring wind
You need to use a micrometer,
You need to have a statistician,
An engineer and an artist to run things.
You can't have a meteorologist
Talking merry gibberish anywhere near.

Spring was never a season, calendar-clear :
There is no discernible shift from
Wind of winter to winds of spring.
It takes maybe a week and a half
From the day you said, this'll never end,
To the day your mind and heart thaw out
To recognize, hey, it's here !
Meanwhile the wind has never stopped.
But once spring's wind comes, it's mostly to stay.
It's like the chinook, only not so urgent.

Spring wind sails over rock ridges
Of snow-cased mountains and swivvies through pines,
Cascades down folds to foothill aspen and prairie sage.
Thus perfumed it sails on out, streams through coulee
Through winter-bleached grass.
A stalk of stubble in the midst of fall's fallow
Waves a greeting and points on north

Where they still wait and doubt still
The coming of spring.

IX. Mountain Breeze

A mountain breeze is a spring wind in space,
A subtle wind without assurance.
It has been warped by its environment :
Rock ridges and northern pines its companions,
Snow its grandma, cold springs its sisters.
It knows rebuff and rejection,
And has never really experienced love.

Therefore one ought not to blame it
For quickly shifting moods and sulks,
For brashness and painful stammers,
As it seethes or sighs in the pines.
When the mountain breeze discovers you
In a high meadow, open to affection,
It's almost immoral in its suggestions.
Other times, in a copse of aspen,
It trembles the leaves with a kind of longing
One cannot stand for long -- feeling so
The same desire for something lasting.

I met it strangely grown, this long-last summer,
Folding cottonwood leaves into brief volumes :
A relentlessness without alpha, omega,
A magnificent river between wide mountains,
Breaking always, ebbing never,
As though an exiled winter day

Were cast adrift in July.
Lord, that longing should so distill,
Mortality be so substantial !
How it shudders us to think
We may be agents, who hardly puff.

But we are strung among the willows for such a playing:
This my score -- faulty retrospect.
(Pearl-gray clouds against more than blue are whiter
 than white.)
Of the three fish I caught, one I threw back.
What of the bird song, descending chimes,
"Riddle, you riddle, you riddle, you riddle " ?

X. Big Wind's a-Growin'

Big wind's a-growin' and the fast clouds are blowin'
The sunset is dyin' and the old house is sighin'
As you come a ridin' with the moon for your guide and
I know it's you, and I know it's true that

>You've come back for me and you've come to stay
>And you'll be my darlin 'til my dyin' day.

Hard rain's a-fallin' and the night owls are callin'
The big creek is swollen and the water comes rollin',
But over the crossin' with your black hair tossin'
I see you wadin' as the moonlight is fadin' and

>You've come back for me and you've come to stay
>And you'll be my darlin' 'til my dyin' day.

The dark storm is goin' and a warm wind is blowin'
Then the sun starts a-risin' in the blue eastern sides and
The wild geese start flyin' as the field birds are cryin'
As you come returnin' with your dark eyes burnin' for

> You've come back for me and you've come to stay
> And you'll be my darlin' 'til my dyin' day.

The sunshine is beatin' on the house and the wheat and
The hot wind is dryin'. The dust starts a-flyin'.
I'm a long time waitin' and you're long time late and
I don't think you're carin' you left my life barren,

> You won't come back for me 'cause you've gone to stay
> And I won't never see you 'fore my dyin' day.

XI. Storm Wind

We were not there when the biggest storm in history hit,
We missed out on all but the aftermath of the million dollar
    wind.
Arking back a day late, we found hail still littering the
    ground
Among the leaves and branches it had mowed.
We went out across the prairie to see the vehicles, bins,
The buildings struck in their four corners
By the wilderness wind among the hailed-out fields.
It had a mythic quality even then, the day after,

Land, Light, Wind and Water

And was hard to believe from the telling, though clear the
   evidence.

But we had seen storms enough of smaller scope or scale,
To become true believers.
We watched from the wide windows of the farmhouse
While another storm wind grabbed an ancient building,
Bouncing it over a reservoir, and were fascinated
Watching another fierce force steadily unzip the roof
Of the nearest Butler bin, knowing we were downwind.
Dad sent us to the basement for the finale.

Perhaps the wind abated a bit, only hurtling the madcap
Twenty foot discus a hundred feet,
Half-way to the house, where it dropped it flat.

The prairie and the wind have a working arrangement :
You don't get in my way, I won't get in yours.
There are few hindrances on the rolling ground, the dipping
   coulees,
No confrontation, no heroics, and no prophetic rebuke.
There are not even trees until we plant them,
Poor orphans, abused all their short lives.
It is man alone who stands against storms, man and the
   mountains,
Which lend a sense of heroic destiny among tattered vapor
   standards.
The farmer feels an unknown urge, a city-building impulse,
(Which he will deny). He surrounds himself with upright
   things,
With trees, with buildings, with old equipment ;
With more buildings -- the farmstead a small ghost city,
Haunted by a jealous family, guarding well their little Babel.

The storm comes, the heavens black with cloud and wind
Breaks the trees, tatters the buildings, and tips the equipment,
While the prairie sits back and watches.
"Shelter-belts" they call trees set in rows against prevailing
    winds.
The best are designed carefully according to species, size and
    density,
To frustrate the steady ocean of air that beats against our
    barks.
But the blasts laugh, and assail the redoubt
As though it were but a great joke,
(No joke to the besieged defenders at all)
Stormy deriders delivering a punchline.

XII. Wind in the Willows

    No one who has had the book read him at an early age
    And lived by a river or played by a stream
    Can pretend to escape sage badger
    Or that sure companion -- water rat ;
    Worthless toad -- beloved for all that ;
    Or the sense of pulling at mole's oars.

    But literature only interprets experience,
    Doesn't make it. The points peculiar,
    The moments particular -- to the universal,
    Disparate -- are the water our oars catch in
    (Though not the current): rehearsals with all
    Their mistakes and memories which lead to the play.

Land, Light, Wind and Water

It was always an argument for providence
That my mother let us play by the river :
Solid evidence some greater than she . . . but I'm adrift.
That's the thing about the willow-wind --
One can hardly lift pen to write,
It takes so little notice of itself.

When we smelled the Willows, we thought not "wind" ;
The breeze was so insubstantial next
The obvious current of opaque power
Flowing by at so much an hour into eternity.
We hardly thought willow, except when we'd happen
Upon a den of those politic creatures, leisurely beavers
(Convincing bone-tired men they are busy !)
The dens, I say, smelled of willow essence
To the point of overpowering, making dizzy
With the fragrance of salicin, a drug they say,
Which drives away infection and rheumatic age.

And out on the river in still boat or canoe
The breeze was only slightly more sensible,
Assuaging the waters, but still incensed toward us
For giving ourselves to apparent streams
Which could of course drown a man,
In different ways than men drown on land.

And Grahame is right, the essential day
Was one with hot sun, but a hint of play
Of wind, just puffs and the smell of willow
So heady, one could go to hell, see Pan,
Or die without knowing what happened,
Not able until afterwards to say.

Land, Light, Wind and Water

The carp and pike and "goldeye" never
Felt or smelled the wind in the willows.
It's strange to think they never will,
Though no doubt the mud and current
Distill some essence to their olfactory equivalents
Filling piscine minds with their own ambivalence.

Our landlocked town sent out sailors,
Three admirals or more -- so the talk along Front Street,
Which faces the river and breathes willow wind,
Attar from cottonwood trees wired at the bases
Against beaver marauders, who prefer willows
But slothfully stoop to other fodder.

The willow-wind blows deep in some souls
Calling them down to docks and shoals,
To decks and berths, to bays and seas --
A mighty call for such a small breeze.
The wind in the willows thinly seems to rejoice
Perhaps with the depth of a still, small voice.

XIII. The Four Winds

To the Blackfoots four was a sacred number, still is to some.
The pipe was offered to the four winds, the compass points
By which we call them -- naming them for their origins
Rather than their destinations.

Land, Light, Wind and Water

The East wind, wind out of the wilderness,
Brought hard times more than once --
To Egypt it brought locusts ;
To Jonah it brought a withering of comfort,
So that he wished to die.
It broke the ships of Tarshish,
And drove back the sea for Israel to pass.
Mr. Jarndyce of Bleak House
Suspected its influences at every bad turn.

The West wind came with mercy
Drove back the locusts from Egypt ;
Our westwind, usually southwest, sometimes brought rain
And life to the thirsty ground ;
But as the song says,
A wayward wind is the westward wind . . .

The North wind, *anemos,* drove rain away,
As we are animated sometimes by a wind,
As an angry face quells a backbiting tongue.
The North wind in Montana is a wind of winter.

Of the South wind few people write or speak,
In Jesus' day it was known for heat.
And a southeast wind stirred up broad waves,
Drove apostolic ships before it.

The four winds are places of scattering,
The prophets set a wide itinerary
For the remnant of Abraham's, God's own people
Into the four winds, the utmost corners.

The four winds are axes of gathering
Which angels range, seeking out the elect,

And when the valley of bones revives,
The spirit and breath will come from the four winds.
"Four strong winds that blow lonely..."
And like the high-running seven seas
Both ebb and flow.

When all things are complete,
The four angels will restrain the winds like horses,
Hold them back from blowing
On earth or sea, from shaking so much as the smallest tree.

XIV. The Windless Times

No one can say they are few, these times without a wind,
Though they don't amount to much,
More like blinks between sightings,
Or the space between raindrops in a deluge.
In the brief warm seasons, there is usually one
When the sunrise boils up
To scour the belly of scaly night,
Then lukes down to a wash
At the opening of business --
When a breeze blows in.
Or in summer after supper when western fires
Are kindled to render essential chrisms.
That calm is unearthly like miraculous prayer.

Land, Light, Wind and Water

The deep of winter has cold days,
Cold enough to freeze the wind,
But not many, for the line is thin,
And it blows like a banshee at snowtime in blizzard.
There are the breeze-days, yes,
But a breeze is a wind.
Who has seen the breeze ?
A few steamy days in the hottest weeks
Support a kind of tropical calm
Where men on machines wish for wind
But cannot have it, no more than water.
And there are calms before storms,
Those brief delicate moments of utter silence
Before the first drops of rain let fall.
They say there is no breeze in hell.

XV. Whirlwind

Out on the dry flats, summer sets its foot down firm.
It stirs up confusion, swirling whirlwinds,
Walking breezes, a kind you can see.
The mornings are fairly calm and cool,
But quickly the blazing blow of light
Bakes up the dew and chalks the dust
For a little gust begging to get up.
Somewhere atop the neighboring hill
As a spot of earth heats its attic air,
A steady breeze pipes it down toward us
In a spin of unequal temper.

Out plowing fields, one sees them best,
For there they snuff up dust like drunkards,
Sucking vats of loose-grain topsoil in,
Into their guts and giddy about.

As summer goes on they increase in size,
In number, too -- often coming in gangs
Of stumbling, wobble-foot, reeling companions,
Circling each other as they spin about.

Dust-born, dervish, bodied wind,
Misfit and mesmerist under the sun.

When the Lord spoke out of the whirlwind
It was Job's first reliable rebuke.

XVI. Night Wind

A youth, I wrote some wallowing verse, dusty with
    sentiment
Which I titled "Wind-song" beginning thus :

"They tell me that your causes are the warm earth and cool
    air
Together making currents strong to blow by like a prayer."

Then a classmate informed me "Windsong" was a perfume

Land, Light, Wind and Water

And I was crushed. A mere concoction for earthly attraction !
What blasphemy. Yet now the verse seems blasphemy to me
Against vague reverence for what poetry is or could be.
Night wind, though the muddy sentiment is dried and
    crackled,
Seems something of poetry's essence.
It means and means, but can't be reduced to meaning.
It sings and sings but can't be called mere singing.
It's beautiful, full of beauty, but not only.
Perhaps allegorizes, analogizes, struggles,
Acts, asserts its existence, is. But none of these alone.
The song "Maria" furnished a tune for those youthless verses,
And probably the theme of angst, but of course,
The wind furnished that to both.
I resented that song as well as loved it.
It was much but could have been so much more.

> *Out here they have a name*
> *For wind and rain and fire*
> *The rain is Tess, the fire is Joe*
> *They call -- the wind -- Maria . . .*

The implication was that "out here" men had
A mystical insight into some deep reality,
Which is absurd. None of us out anywhere do,
Not natively, not reliably. Perhaps Ma-RYE-uh was a demon.
The night wind is a guardian angel, a lullabier,
A maintenance man, keeping the world though we're
    exhausted.

In ninth grade I wrote some lines
In response to an English class assignment
To produce an example of simile.

Land, Light, Wind and Water

> The wind blew like a patient giant
> Doing his last job,
> Picking up the leaves one by one
> And carrying them gently toward the river.

I received my first high, mind-reeling plaudit
When the teacher accused me of plagiarism.
"What book did you get this out of?" he asked.
And I was unable to defend myself,
Or thank him, not knowing which.

The lonely farmer whose wife has left him for a sprucer
May not hear any promise in the night wind,
May hear mockery, despair, and self-destruction
Whistling around the corners,
But he sees the same message in a sunny day
And in the roses beside his door.
The night wind would comfort him,
Would woo him back to life and meaning
If he would listen and let it.

There is a patient giant quality to it,
Especially in the fall, for patience is the virtue
Most needing then. Tribulation worketh patience
And the expectation of tribulation moreso.
It lumbers forward, always forward,
Without an ounce of subterfuge,
Picking up what's left lying about
And sweeping it on, one broomstroke -- another,
Allowing the leaf or scrap to lodge
Against a stone, a trunk, a tuft,
A little while, then carries it on.
Like poetry, the night wind serves to scour
Odd, accumulated bits from the landscape.

Land, Light, Wind and Water

XVII. Cloud-Driver

High above the common atmospheres of earth
The cloud-driver runs, may never cease,
Running on, perhaps, when there are no clouds,
Perhaps so steady as to connote peace,
But fast -- when the clouds are there they race
Like ships on course, headed home light-laden
Or prairie schooners, new Conestogas
Bearing hopes of many: man, matron, maiden.

The sky itself seems marching by,
A flotilla for a new world on surge of sea,
Pioneers heading west by southwest :
Stately, benign, bound for the lea --
Eternity or bust, gray in the dusky light
Above these mountain sprouts --
There are yet no shadows of any doubts ;
They will journey on all through this night.

XVIII. Windmill

The windmill bears a presumptuous name,
Like most things men manufacture --
Like automobiles and constitutions
It does not begin to meet its promise.

Land, Light, Wind and Water

The mills of the gods grind exceedingly fine,
But our windmills are small crude things,
Usually pumping but a little water
To feed a small herd or water a garden.

Yet they are like harps hung on the willows,
Aeolian nets to catch the wind's tail,
And stand out bravely against a horizon
Harvesting wind for some purpose at least.

The one in my mind is annealed by a lens,
A photograph I took once at sunset.

A camera shot and a poet's throw
Both capture so little of what's to show,
So very little of what is and what passes,
What blows beyond the mill and the grasses.
The mill grabs a little, all in vanes,
Through crank or gears turns its pains
Down a shaft to a small-minded machine
Producing what can scarcely mean.

    I am but a rusty windmill
        whirling dry and chafing tunes,
    Driven by the earnest wind
        which all around me sifts the dunes.

    Once I drew the darkling waters
        from a hidden well below ;
    Now my only task is pointing
        this the way the wind should blow.

Land, Light, Wind and Water

Painted once in shiny green,
    I fade and chip to red and brown.
Birdnests, once in all my angles,
    all have tumbled to the ground.

Dunes rub backs against my braces,
    gusts fling sand against my vanes.
On I'm driven, never resting,
    whisp'ring songs without refrains.

Something yet goes singing through me
    as I creak out unoiled sighs,
Motivated like the clouds
    that rush unresting through these skies.

Light of evening sends my shadow
    through a plot where five graves lie.
Long years past they all were tended;
    other shadows slanted by.

Dry years come and bearings wear,
    mills and men give up their grist.
All things end, both hope and care;
    only winds blow as they list.

Sometimes faintly blows a promise –
    soil untroubled, crops grown high,
Deep wells rung by hidden waters
    from some fountain never dry.

I am but a rusty windmill
    whirring dry and chafing tunes,
Driven by the earnest wind
    which all around me sifts the dunes.

Windmills like weathervanes do not last.
Many a tower stands bald to the blast
Without its wheel of whirring blades,
Fallen long since among the shades.
A mill needs more anointing than it usually gets.
And when God speaks out of the whirlwind,
The mill spins wildly or comes to a stop,
That being just the sort of wind it can't reap,
Except in stillness and silence.

XX. *Three Persons of the Wind*

Among the persons in the wind, there is one
Like an old aunt talking high and thin,
As though long accustomed to addressing herself,
Using words in public taken off a shelf,
Saying things we already know in a crotchety way.

Another there is, a brother who died,
Who was lost in the war, who was crucified,
And is rumoured risen --
But except in old letters
He never speaks -- our hearts long
As the barn roof creaks.

And one who sounds always, in sighs, in moans
In the deepest of wordless heart-borne groans
With a constancy to which we can't quite cotton
For when we are steeled, we feel best-forgotten ;
We don't want the comfort of your scandalous hope.

Land, Light, Wind and Water

XXI. The North Wind's Doorstep

She never can go in,
Can barely crawl that far.
And she who can't go home again
Roars foreign and afar.

There, she knows, dwell many
Her hyperborean kin,
In sunshine and abundance,
But they cannot let her in.

Those dear ones do not hate her.
They think her lot the best,
But she who knows both world and home
Knows which of them are blessed.

XXII. Profits Shall Become Wind

My accountant promises my days are numbered,
Weighed like the winds he brings out of his vault,
Weighed and found wanting by all calculations,
Passing away like Job's -- as a weaver's shuttle,
My life is a wind, my soul pursued with terrors,
And my welfare fleeing like a cloud.

Land, Light, Wind and Water

It is still a jolt of mind to me,
A speed bump to my modernity that God deigns --
That God deigns to breathe, to fly, to walk
On the wings of the wind (though the wind
Is wholesome, cleansing sun and moon of clouds,
Driving the chaff and dust before it)
For wind is like flesh, passing away
And never coming again -- not that one.

It would be more comprehensible
If wind-in-his-fists had merely driven,
Pursued the noisome breezes, rending our walls,
Withering our leaves, or carried storm and flood --
Troubling his own house, who inherited but
       whirlwinds.

That the boisterous gale be calmed, the floods,
The wavering waves, tossed to and fro, find rest,
When even stars fell like windblown figs, untimely,
Disconcerts, frightens, frankly scares me.

Or perhaps I might be able to affirm
A reed shaken by the wind, an oracular messenger.

That the swift wind should bear us on its wings,
When we would rather snuff little wild-ass breaths,
Build houses on sand with untempered mortar,
Than be snatched by a contrary lord-over-winds --
We would rather gather in our unwashed rags around
Our windy molten mysteries, hide from the oasis.
Where can we hide from our hiding?
Is there shadow of rock in this weary land --
Who shall be a hiding place from the wind,
And a covert from the tempest?

Land, Light, Wind and Water

Ah, but he who boasts of a large gift
Is like clouds and wind without rain.

XXIII. Fall Wind

Thank God the crops are in the barn,
Or sold and hauled away from harm.
The wind's commenced to blow, and it's fall for sure.
There's still seed to go in the ground,
But except for the worry of getting into the field,
The weather can't hurt us anymore this year.

Sough, sough, sow the wind . . . and reap . . .

We should be happy, rest assured,
But there's great uneasiness in the wind of fall.
We know where it leads -- bitter cold, snow,
But we don't know when, and we fear to know,
We fear other things lasting longer than winter
The body's frost, dissolution of sinner.

There is no sadness like the sadness of fall,
No wanderlust, no wilderness call,
No longing for better, no wish for end,
No sharper sense of wanting a friend.
Nor any briefer, brighter joys.

There is no essence of fall like the wind,
Not the smell of smoke, not the grains we've ginned,
Not the geese in the sky, not the fields of stubble,
Not the kids in school, not the old folks' trouble.

Fall wind is a juggernaut of force
Going on for weeks, never changing course.
Sometimes diminishing the space of an hour
Only to return with redoubled power.

And when it blows it speaks . . .

XXIV. What the Wind Said

Comes a day when the wind has blown a week or two
And winter crops are nigh sown, that we know it isn't
Mere physical causes, not just noises, but words and clauses
Being enunciated through the wires and around the corners
Of houses and byres.

And at first we deny it and shake our heads,
Half-smiling at what we thought it said,
And that we thought it, the joke on us for imagining such;
Much mental fuss -- I must be getting old, or crazy
Or need to go to town.

But ere winter has come full and furious,
We no longer think our ears delirious, we listen instead,

Land, Light, Wind and Water

Gradually intently to what the wind said, trying to tell
What it meant and what, if anything, we should reply
To the one in the ocean passing by.

It squeals past the window crack and drops to a hiss,
First rebuking our blocked ears that would not listen
To its siren screaming (fire this time?)
Or acknowledge it earlier, then begins to intone
Analyses of our hearts in a moan.

It drones the decalogue like a jug-band player.
This un-hyperventilating sooth-sayer understates,
But states again and again, we likewise have broken
All of the ten. Or if one point only, it slurs and sighs,
Still guilty of all, and no one replies.

You're unhappy a treble trill under the eave
Choruses. Don't let your snug house deceive you
Into claiming otherwise based on what is seen.
This it punctuates by rattling the screens and finding
One uncaulked crack, flowing in the unseen track.

Your hopes are empty around chimneys squeaks
As successive gusts leapfrog the peak to the lea,
Where the snap of landing sounds the shingles' flap.
A whistle signals work's end, something final,
Or a slow train coming fast -- or already past.

You've settled for less than your birthright sounds
From somewhere in the wind's wide bounds, but the swish
Of the scanty trees near the house was not the voice ;
Nor loose panes in the basement door, nor a hundred other
      loci more.

None of these was the source of what the wind said,
But a pneuma-nous numinous voice in your head,
In your heart, in your soul -- You need grace.

And in the wind's ebb, through the briefest lull,
Someone not wind said I fill full.

XXV. Things in the Wind

Blown about by every wind, unstable objects of little weight
Constitute the mail and freight, the detritus out on the sea
With no destination but the everlasting lea
Or maybe the back of the wind.
They may wear away to nothing first,
For the wind is not a careful carrier,
Dropping each package every few yards or kicking each,
Or pitching it hard against rock, tree or building.
The airmail escapes such treatment, of course -- the clouds
Stay high on fast winds like the wicked, but fruitless ones
Shedding no rain, hastening on leaving nothing behind.
And waves, too, fare somewhat better, although like men of
      little faith,
They are driven and tossed to a foam and lather, without
      wisdom.
But the main material burdens of wind are dust and chaff,
The occasional weed, tumbling before the prince of the power
      of the air

Land, Light, Wind and Water

Working in the children of disobedience, dropping seed
All along its path to destruction.
And these, too, are susceptible to simile, the dust and chaff
Like the unbelieving, who deny their motion has any
    significance,
Borne they insist purely by chance and bound, they assure us,
Toward the common small fate of all things, an endless lull
    insensate.

Dust in the wind was once mud: a first blowing found it
    sapped
With blood and firm and planted as a place of growing, a
    fertile soil
For rooting and knowing significance, producing fruit, like
    hearing
Something true and in truth enduring to the point one
    couldn't forget.
Chaff and stubble, the dross of threshing, too, sail away in the
    air.
The seed is separated, no one cares what becomes of them,
Except themselves, and their fellows -- not compassionately,
    but
Out of reflective self-sympathy, fearing common doom,
Which makes for the imitation empathetic gloom of the
    godless.

The North Wind tried to tell Diamond how it was, that those
    before her
Were driven and tossed like waves of the sea
For purposes beyond both the two of them
(Evil nurses and crossing sweepers, too). But the latter
    would one day
Find they had come to the North Wind's back, everlasting
    home,

Land, Light, Wind and Water

While those who never gave in to the wind, would perish before her,
As though in sin.
And, not literally flung about in the sky, not in our county,
Where no tornadoes sigh, but just driven and tossed as the dust,
Men and women, boys, girls, mind-mussed and harried, unable to rest,
Are battered before the wind's cold breast; which they imagine
But an agent of shove, not of warmth, of flowing milk, or of love.
In their bleak houses in their bleak hearts, the wind seems always in the east.
Not the least comfort they find, but only a sense that they and all things
Are driven hence in insignificance, unless somehow they
Can cast their own anchor, sew their own dress, their own windbreak,
Which will make them kings of their own flake of chaff,
Give a kind of meaning each to his mote.
Some there are, giving all that up, who know the wind,
And their own lack, who go to dwell at its back,
For it's not fish sense majesty in oceans vast,
But they who go down to the sea in ships,
The awestruck sailor on the back of the sea.
And when the trees bow down their heads,
The wind comes past.

> "A boy's will is the wind's will,
> And the thoughts of youth are long, long thoughts."
> -- Henry Wadsworth Longfellow

Land, Light, Wind and Water

THE SOUND OF MANY WATERS

Altissima quaeque flumina minimo sono tabi
("The deepest rivers flow with the least sound")
Quintus Curtius, VII, 4, 13

I. Come to the Waters

Ho, everyone who thirsts, come to the waters . . .
It's not as simple as it once was :
If you'd come to drink
You ought to know about Giardia and dioxin
And a few other modern ingredients.
Nevertheless come to the waters.
These waters, at least, are always roiled,
And if they are dirty
To the point we sometimes fear they are spoiled forever,
Do not therefore refuse to come.
Mere potability is not the only question
Providing your thirst is not merely biological.
(If it is, go ahead, drink -- other animals are drinking.)

Your coming, my coming are acknowledgments of something
 more:
That something essentially good is free, freely offered
And flowing down -- not by our design --

From high springs, to fast, frothed streams,
To creeks fish-full and winding through prairie
To this river, which will not stop (not a second) for us
But hurries on to its place of receiving,
Of being received fully, not just a bit
As we receive it. So come, and look.
Give yourself time to see through the silt
Or refuse of man and storm,
For we all thirst, for something lasting,
For water to end all panting of heart.
Yes, come to the waters and think . . .

II. Spring Water

In this city of our sojourn it comes in plastic bottles.
But long before I imagined such contradictions possible
I played beside a spring, went there on high afternoons
With my father and mother to watch pure waters well.
That spring was archetypical -- Giant Springs,
Said to be the largest freshwater spring in the world --
Blurting out volumes of clean water,
Willing its liquid life to the muddy river
From bank of which it surged day and night.
Pure beds of watercress swayed in its depths
(There my Dad stooped to pick a sprig,
Gave me my first taste of the cool hot stuff).

Land, Light, Wind and Water

There was a semi-arid Eden built around the springs,
Of grassy slopes and flying-fuzz cottonwood trees --
Which memory peoples with parents and kin.
There was also a hatchery,
With tanks of big trout, haunted by albinos.

The river did not begin at the spring.
It flowed by through dams which rode the Great Falls,
Like toads perched on princes,
Desecrating yet another God-given beauty ;
But the undammed river was already wide,
Having sources afar -- the Gallatin, the Madison and the
        Jefferson,
With many others pouring in their oblations
Before it reached Giant Springs and the Falls.

Like the archetypical archetype,
Giant Springs was atypical in some of its ways.

Typical springs abound in the mountains,
Often but trickles out of the rocks,
Or tiny pools welling out of sod
On high prairie against steep slopes.
From them came smallest, but steadiest streams,
(Only direst drought could dry them up).
But giant or tiny, one could drink from a spring,

Reach down with cupped hand and drink deep and free,
Of water always cold, tasteless -- so pure,
And feel some agreement spring up in oneself.

The true sources of all rivers are springs,
Springs, rain and snow: pure waters all
At the beginning anyway.

And when other waters above ground are frozen,
Springs -- seeming coldest -- yet flow free,
Winter's warmest: constant waters.

III. *Mountain Snows*

Our mountains wear venerable nightcaps late into summer,
Making the melting-myth of glacial ages look likely,
But except on the high divide, no snow lasts all year --
And even there the glaciers are dwindling.
Snow melts -- and in its melting produces the most lovely
Of mountain waters. "Minerals," they say
But the word won't suffice, nor any analysis
Of the deep blues and jaded greens in snow-melt lakes.

Snows melt and run down, water alpine plants, soon
    flowered ;
But also our poor crops in semi-aridity,
Root-tongues panting but for a drop.
Snow's the most part of our bare moisture,
Usually waters more grain than even spring showers.

He is privy to something who walks the mountains at
    snowfall :
In the real mountains, not those pseudo-Swiss, semi-citied,
See-me suave scenes of skis and sweaters.
A few times, near Christmas, climbing up after trees,
We watched the gray cover suddenly blanch,

Land, Light, Wind and Water

Blanket forest and hearts with light made material
More like pure idea than anything ought to be.
A spring-fed mountain stream among the drifts is like . . .
An orchestra in a shell; a children's parade; a saint's
    procession,
Tripping down, running, announcing advent :
An arrival of beauty all-embracing, transforming.
Some places the accumulation (so fast in the mountains)
Covers the torrent: only a muffled chuckle gives sign.
Its existence is unpleasant to otherwise discover.

If the snow ceases, the clouds pass, the sun explodes
And makes the creeks seem black amidst snow,
Crystal reflections blinding, beating hot against eyes' backs
At mystifying contrast to the cold tactility, biting touch.

But by late June the snow is gone from the mountains,
Even from the stony ravines of the north slopes --
It all runs down the creeks and streams,
Joying the trout with its coldness, the caddisflies with its
    purity,
And the rivers below with its substance.

IV. Cloudbursts

The rain seldom surprised us,
Giving always half an hour's notice,
But we weren't always ready, even though we knew.
The best that pours out of the sky
Sometimes is inconvenient, poor timing by our calculations.

To give up little tasks not quite complete
In the middle because crop-making, life-supporting rain
Is come in pounding curtains is not pleasant
If you have a one-track mind. We all did.
There is so little total rain on our relatively wet plateau
(Relative to other parts of the county)
That every quarter inch is a flood of significance :
Is something to be thankful for in the abstract.
In the concrete -- which is where the rain fell one time
I was manufacturing a basketball court --
It may rain howls and bitches.

It puddles dust into mud and runs awhile
Across the ground so dry as to be foreign,
As though it were powdered oil or wax,
Until the earth remembers and opens up
To receive the long-besought sky's tears ;
And replies with odors rich and fair,
The smell of wet soil, always surprising
Because it is so good and so well hidden.

V. By the Rivers of Babylon

The river above town is a source of life,
Below, it carries off death.
All that we need comes from above,
All we discard, flows away.
Therefore river-dwellers everywhere
Contend with the scourings and sluice
Of towns above and send theirs on.

Land, Light, Wind and Water

The rivers flow east, but we are repaid,
Repaid double for all our sins.
Babylon, the great city
Sits on many rivers and defiles the flow,
Sending out its corrupted riches,
The pollution of its harlotry toward every source.
We sing for her: it is her presses,
Her moneys that enslave us,
Bid us make merry with old home tunes.

Water brings life and death :
Water-borne bacteria and chemicals kill ;
The water-built business and farm feed ;
Water for beavers, water for mining,
Water for lumbering, water for power ;
And water to carry up and back
The taxman and taxes,
The empire's men and tributes,
In exchange for far-borne fatal diseases
Of soul as well as body.

We are broken and in chains.
Oh, Jerusalem, the heavenly city,
Will I forget you? Will I forget your beauty ?
Will you send me hope on your clean waters ?
Oh, Lord, do not destroy Babylon.
No, do not requite her according to her iniquities.
Send her washing waters of life.

VI. *The Rain In the Leaves*

I hear the rain coming down in the leaves
And it sounds like the bells in the town.
The soft mist comes close. Like a sorrowing ghost
It wanders the streets up and down.

The river is running away
The long night is turning to day,
And I hear the rain coming down.

I see the moon rushing on through the clouds.
First it hides, then it glows, then it shines.
I hide my light, too, but it never breaks through --
Not in words, not in looks, not in signs.

Why should I hide what I feel ?
Is a feeling hidden still real ?
And I hear the rain coming down.

I'm alone by the stream, it runs on and I dream ;
Still it pulls -- though untied, love still binds.
I wish I could be as unmoved as the trees
As the oak, and the birch and the pine.

But the river carries me along
I take nothing on but a song,
And I hear the rain coming down.

VII. Rivulets

Rivulets look insignificant; the word sounds so,
A diminutive -- but the life of the body is in the blood
Seeping through capillaries as well as flooding the heart.
The effluence of the minute spring
Or the infinitesimal melting of a snowdrift
Becomes a life-giver from moment of birth.
It trickles over and splashes the lichen, locked to rock --
The orange, black or mustard green creature,
Itself the slowest life on the mountain:
Its algae soul sucks in wet, beginning to stir,
Make its seasonal slow sustenance.
The tiny moss plants soak and distill earth and air
Along the trickling life-spill, exhaling soilly smells.
And the deep-rooted sage and Engelman spruce,
Then the aspens and cottonwoods, and myriad flowers:
Yellowbells, asters, saxifrage, salsify all swell and bud
With the rivulet's blood, running on, over, undiminished.

VIII. As the Deer Longs for the Flowing Stream

>As the deer longs for the flowing stream
>So longs my heart for Thee.
>As the deer longs for the flowing stream
>So longs my heart for Thee.
>My soul thirsts for God, for the living God,
>When shall I come and behold Thee ?

Land, Light, Wind and Water

IX. *Shonkin Creek*

Shonkin Creek, Chanson, Chantierre -- song or woodyard
Or an unknown boatman -- Frenchman, Englishman,
    Chinaman --
Or maybe an old Blackfoot word mumbled into English --
None now knows -- too old and familiar --
Like other questions we ask too late.

Emerging from eastern edge of western mountains,
It flows from the Highwood range,
Then meanders down to the young Missouri.
Born high at the junction of two creeks,
Both springfed from the heads of valleys,
It descends quickly through a broader defile,
Wearing bed boulders to a deep-cut canyon
Before leaping out into the Big Sag,
Broad flat valley reputed by some the river's old path.

The Big Sag and its prairie are to Shonkin Creek
As a clearing is to a worldwise deer --
After leaping out, it becomes very cautious.
The native trout sense the difference of temper
And stay in the mountains, hook-jawed with wisdom.

But perhaps it would be more accurate to say,
Shonkin Creek has two faces, -- or grows old quickly.
In the mountains the stream is active, impetuous,
Down below it grows quickly lethargic:
Up in the rocks and canyons -- headlong;
But wandering, listening in the widelands below.
The mountain stream is clear and cold;
Yet in the valley is soon grown muddy,
A drain in the prairie for stormy alluvium.

Land, Light, Wind and Water

In a dry summer, Shonkin Creek follows suit,
Leaving rocky beds, pools and higher beaver dams
Thick-bordered with nettles and mint.
Down below its earthly remains are a mud-cracked path
Back and forth through fly-haunted willows,
With a few rotting pools where carp and bullheads
Challenge sun and heat-beating time
In a race to unexpected rain.
The fish often lose.

Higher up the creek smells pine and sage,
Below it's overwhelmingly willow - beaver perfume.
And since it was the closest stream to forested land
From the river's highest steamboat port,
Woodcutters early found its sources,
Where, singing their many wide-water songs,
They denuded the slopes for fire-box fuel,
Floating it down or driving ox-team loads
Back to the boiler-built town on the river.

Shonkin Creek is a neighbor, like others:
Well behaved, pleasant most of the time,
But breaking out every decade or so
In a hooligan flood to enrage or puzzle.
Then it settles and flows its new bed:
More to be trusted now, or less ?
Still it has never fought a water rights battle,
And bears mountain waters, a salver to the sea.

X. The Dipper

'Twas with my grandfather and cousins I first saw an ouzel,
On a family expedition full of sturm and drang
Back when time was wider than the mountains.
It flew from a cleft beneath a waterfall
Where twice descended winter water hid its nest.

Another time I saw an ouzel spring from a rock,
Gray-brown, and incontinent with life,
Bobbing in the dance which bought its name.
Dipping and bowing, it leapt and disappeared
Beneath overwhelming floods
Rushing toward apocalyptic rivers.

The last time I saw an ouzel,
My wife and I skirted a broken cliff
Along a path too easy for the mountains,
When doubtful evening cut enthusiasm to the quick.
Uncertainly we turned and made our way back down
Along the split rock stream
Which led unerringly to our camp and beyond.
We saw the dipper, heard its thin cry,
Dipper and sharer in our paths and fears,
Wandering from rock to log among flotsam,
Skipping on water-covered stone.

Water ouzel, Dipper,
Bird of water, rock and air,
Deep diver, bottom walker,
Partner in life amidst these mountains.

XI. Beaver Ponds and Muskrat Tunnels

Two creatures living in or on the water
Effect its flow more than any others --
Not otters for all their joy,
Not fish for their single-mindedness,
But the sturdy mammals, eager beaver,
And little cousin, muddy muskrat.
One builds, the other tears down,
Like yin and yang of the rodent family.
Both have undergone serious persecution
(Yesterday's beaver hats, today's muskrat jackets).
The beaver cannot cease to build;
The muskrat must burrow --
So they hinder master man, master-minding his frustration.
Mountain creeks, prairie streams, despite man's plans, his
    ambitions,
Are often chains of terraced ponds by beaver engineering.
The best mountain swimming (not best fishing)
Was always "at the beaver dam," deep quiet waters.
But down on the prairie, where we swam in reservoirs,
Man-built coulee-choking sloughs,
The other rodent does demolition.
A dam unattended, let go to grass
Will soon be honey-combed with burrows.
Muskrat tunnels it, he and his kits
Dig holes at waterline around the water;
Making no distinction for the dam man built him
Until a good storm washes out the back wall,
Empties the water leaving but a mudhole.
Beavers and muskrats are both compulsive,
Minor juggernauts, bent upon doing.
Break a beaver dam -- soon it will be mended,
Build a man dam -- soon muskrat - rended.

But come at dusk to a pond, a reservoir,
Sit still wearing lots of sharp mosquito dope.
See whiskered heads cut silent through water,
Carrying willow leaves, or sticks for dam or nesting,
Cruising in mirror-peace, seeming almost aimless --
And it will make you pause and ask, which of us is driven ?
Which creature fights the flow, which breaks the barriers --
Fills up or empties out wisdom or water ?

XII. Lakes

We have no lakes worth mentioning east of the mountains --
Fort Peck and Tiber Dam are just big reservoirs.
(Few real lakes have been made by men.)
My parents began their marriage at a mountain lake,
In a log cabin on idyllic shores.

The name Swan Lake was thus linked to "honeymoon"
Which I early heard, such a cosy word.
We went back there every summer while I was small:
Pete and I learned to swim and dive off the dock;
I learned to fish and row a boat in circles.
For my father it was a reminder, a poor substitute,
For the distant shore of his boyhood Atlantic.

A lake is a gathering together, a temporary place,
A longing to remain, a reticence.
A lake is a watery rough equivalent of a life:

Land, Light, Wind and Water

Streams flow in, a river flows out.
In between -- an illusion of permanence barely achieved.

After a few years, we began to go to Seeley Lake,
As much, I always thought, because my mother was Lucille,
As for any other reason.
There I got the worst sunburn of my life,
Wading for hours in the shallows
Trying to catch the sun's fish.
(I lay in the tent for two days -- moaning.)
There my father told me -- we'd been offered a boat --
That it's always better not to borrow things.
I could not understand it, too much the poet.

A lake is a place for contemplation,
A place of pleasant things to look at,
But also a place to see oneself --
To gaze at length at one's reflection
In clear waters and in others lives --
Eye-green water, eyes, words, and souls.
The last lake we went to was named Holland --
Weed-grown the summer we were there:
The first place I challenged a stretch of water,
Swimming a hundred yard wide bay
And seeing my life flash by three times
Before dropping on the shore.

A lake is for learning limitation --
Shores, bounds, to creatures and creation:
The bordering walls of we are and can,
And a body of water surrounded by land.

Land, Light, Wind and Water

XIII. Dry Year

A dry year is a year when fifteen inches of moisture
Dwindles down to five or ten.
In a dry year everybody relaxes,
Does less and worries more --
Sometimes there is no need to harvest.
But a dry year gives a clearer sense of hell
And makes a wet year seem more like heaven.

XIV. Farm Laborer Drowned

Parched by the unrelenting sun
He other times had basked in,
Earth-streaked gory-gray in dust
From which he or his master
Hoped to raise a crop,
The farm laborer ended day
With a plunge from a muddy shore
Into a weed-webbed pool
Of stored-up bitter water,
And died from the shock.
That reservoir he knew as good
From other plunges, divers times,
When he had leaped and crossed,
Exulting, through cool and lyey brine.
Seeped salts matter not a lick
To those who look for life to water.
He did not count back-burning labor,
Temple-beating roar of chores

A new item in the balances of time,
They seemed to him right burdens.
Nor did he know how thoroughly
His muddy sweat anointed him
To die in that refreshing.

Some one pulled his pallid body
From the land-leeched depths,
And laid him last in damp soil.
At least the crop was planted.

XV. Hebgen Lake -- 1959

An uncanny movement on the face of the deep
Shivered through air, water, clay and tree.
Clung couples snuffled, fear flew through tents,
As rose giant tremors, stalked to and fro
Marrying themselves to flesh and blood.
The great stone began to roll.
Scattered thoughout the sorry vale
Strangers and aliens felt flimsy folds shake,
Heard groans of creation, longing to escape.
Sharp echoes trumpeted against high walls.

Profligate grace, earth-filling, tower-building
For all people, all creatures, came to a halt.
Perhaps an inaccurate estimate, improper accounting,
Speculations arose about corruption in high places.

At the far corners of the state we felt the coming
Devastation, noumenous in rattled cups and panes.
As some cried, mountains down upon them
Thrust freely under other knees,
The great stone ran up the far slope
Like an escaping spy, and poised there.

XVI. *Navigable River*

From St. Louis to a few miles below Great Falls
The Missouri was once navigable,
Meaning boats carrying hundreds of tons
Could ply that stretch in spring or mid-summer
In a good year, if the pilot was sharp, and the owners lucky.

Navigable is a relative sort of term,
For if iron bars don't make a prison,
A few major dams don't impede navigation.
If dreams and imaginations go aground,
It isn't on sandbars or concrete pylons.
The dams were built, of course,
After "navigation" faded out at the turn of the century.
The railroads killed the steamboat trade,
And the dams stone the grave:
Tiber, Fort Peck, Garrison, Oahe,
Big Bend, Fort Randall, Gavins Point --
Examples of human government short in sight,

Land, Light, Wind and Water

Military engineers at their most mediocre.
But the river does not stop for dams,
Not though reservoirs take forty years to fill,
Not though (perhaps in a hundred years) silt fill them up,
Leaving barren flood-plain terraces.
The river itself continues to navigate.
So do the minds of small boys in river towns
All along those myriad miles of bank, bluff and prairie
Boys on homemade rafts, in canoes and kayaks,
Old men in rowboats, pontoon floats and speedboats.

The river is still navigable far beyond its old limits,
Now we have crack pilots to guide through new-tried waters,
Captain H. Finn and the partners Mole and Ratty ;
Those travelers Marlowe and trader Kurtz
To warn of the horror at both ends of the river.
We've songs, ballads, musicals and musicians, old and new :
Shenandoah, Ole Man River, Red River Valley,
Moon River, The Water is Wide, and Loch Lomond,
All those great-heart Jordan songs,
Songs like Deep River :

> -- *My home is over Jordan,*
> *Deep river, Lord, I want to cross over into campground.*

Navigable I should say so !
Traffic churns the waters today: paintings, tales and novels,
Even gold-panning poems, dragged up by keelboat ;
Making their Lewis and Clarkish way up into the purchase,
The "Great American Desert" where natives are outlandish.
Twain's Mississippi as well as the boy-books,
Other fogbound sailors, Whitman to Eliot.
And older passages open -- back through wide waters
To deep streams pouring out of England, Ireland, Scotland.

Yes, the river's navigable to those who never see it,
As well as to those who burrow beside it.

XVII. Late-Watch Song of a Landlocked Sailor

Away I go, said he to me,
Away across the churning sea,
Where the white waves wash the rising prow
And old man moon has a misty brow.

I'm off he whispered in my ear,
Where the rain falls like a maiden's tear,
Where the children reach and touch the stars,
And the red crab plays on the sandy bars.

I'm gone he called through the thinning fog,
Where canaries sing with the green tree frog,
Where the gull flies high and the cod swims deep
And the breezes lull a man to sleep.

He's gone I told the pillar piles
Where an old man's days don't count the miles
Where a man can't do a bit of wrong,
And the strong sea sings a churning song.

Land, Light, Wind and Water

XVIII. Kingfisher

Blue as blood of heaven without cloud
The kingfisher sits lightly on his throne,
Rules stream and pond, river and lake,
With the dignity of Japan's Emperor :
Unsupported by arms, alone with his bride,
His bearing remains unbowed, his crown sure.
I have seen kingfisher, solitary bird,
Hurry from branch to distant tree,
Long time linger, gazing down
Into the depths of his domain ;
Heard him descend from that high limb,
Death-rattle and plunge
Relentless to his deep victim.
The cold catch he spares not,
Carries home to his dark cave,
Tunnel-tomb for the smooth-caught creature
Brown sepulchre full of life,
Children, fishers and kings.
Gone kingfisher again, seeking another
To bury in warm life,
Once more to descend with the sword of his mouth
To make good the broad claim of his name.

XIX. Muddy Waters

The Missouri ran muddy as far back as records tell.
When I grew up some of it was sewage,
But it was always something.

They say the preponderance of mud in the Mississippi
Comes from the "Mighty Mo" -- and therefore
The delta may be midwest real estate.
Silt, oxides, alkali salts, gumbo, Bentonite, what-have-you,
The river has always been what you call semi-liquid :
" The best water in the world for your jaw " ;
" The paddlewheels stirred up dust in a low year " ;
" Too thick to pour, too thin to plow ",
And a thousand other wry lines to the river's credit.

Much of its mystery would be gone without
The tan-brown pigment roiling in suspension.
The Blackfoots revered "underwater creatures",
Mythical animals of huge size and powers
Thought to lurk in the turgid depths.
Even in backwaters or bar-borne pools where settling
    occurs
The mildest disturbance raises the particulate,
Muddies the waters, veiling the bottom, currents and
    purposes.
There is a lot of gold -- and a lot of history
Hidden under all that mud, that waterborne curtain.
They extract most of the sediment
In the water they give us for drinking,
But there's no filter fine enough to remove the mystery.

XX. Triple Divide (Rivers Come Down)

A single drop of water drawn by the sun
From the Aleutian breakers or Bering Sea

Land, Light, Wind and Water

Or the Sea of Japan, having sailed the sky
As highblow drift or more newly spawned
In Canadian waterfalls or Alaskan tides
Condenses out of the warm wet wind
Which braved the Cascades and flows over the Rockies
Falling at the nexus of the continent --
A single drop of rain or dew set on the pinnacle
Of North America -- not the highest point,
But the place corresponding most nearly
To that mythical high explorer's quest :
The mid-most height, place of Northwest passage.
A drop of water on Triple Divide
Separates infinitesimal and begins to move
In three directions, into three watersheds,
Toward three remote ends.

One third drop moves down the west face
Joins the trickles feeding tiny streams
Gorging little torrents plunging to Nyack,
The creek which grows among the mountains
To the Middle Fork of the Flathead River.
West it winds to the Flathead, itself,
Then south to southwest, then northwest again,
Down widening valleys to Clark Fork,
To the Pen d'Oreille and then the Columbia ;
Whence it swells with international waters
Bound again south by tortuous ways along the Cascades ;
At last again west to the wide mouth,
It pours out its tons of fresh into salty,
The Pacific Ocean.

One third of the drop seeps to the north,
Joins afternoon melt from late summer snowpack,
Courses singing down among bare rocks and lichens

To a foot-wide stream cold and clear as crystal
Through a high basin to a stream shooting faster
To Red Eagle Creek, through its hanging lake
And on to the valley lake, long St. Mary's,
Deep and blue-watered, thence it flows again
In St. Marys River by cold affinity bound due north
To Oldman's River, heart of Blackfoot country,
Into South Saskatchewan, bearing northeast
And the Saskatchewan, into Lake Winnepeg.
Then out it surges, winding lakes to the Nelson,
Bound for the great ancient fur-traders' haven,
Hudson Bay, on the edge of
The Arctic.

The drop's other third steals from the escarpment
Toward the east, sliding south of the curving ridge
And joins others melting in small cataracts
Dropping into the deep glacial valley,
Collecting in pine-set, blue basin lakes,
Sources of the North Fork of Cut Bank River,
Flowing east to Marias, quickly borne to the plains,
Which joins the Teton, soon joining the Missouri.
Thence across two thousand miles southeast,
To the Mississippi, pathway of nation,
Rolling on south to warm climes, and the Delta,
Into the Gulf, great bay of
The Atlantic.

A single drop of water, a single shower,
Gone three ways so diverse, no one could predict it,
No one untutored in high peak topography.

Land, Light, Wind and Water

XXI. Surfaces and Bends

The pilots read the waters, as you've heard from Clemens,
Each looked down from his high wheelhouse
On the waters flowing -- hither or thence,
And read not the depths (no magicians' tricks)
But charts, memory, banks, and surface.
The river has a skin, a rippling hide
That shows up its muscles, any bones inside:
Shallows, snags, bars and rocks --
The surface shows all to a seeing man,
To a man with the call.
But to the rest of us the surface of the water lies,
Makes suffering look sensual, throws mud in our eyes.
The best-looking water is the worst to navigate.
The water looking deepest is where your keel grates.
Snags and sawyers lurk ever unlikely,
Ever bound down, poised to strike on the way.

Yet there's not a pilot reads
The water around the next bend --
Not even a pilot with a Huckleberry friend.

XXII. Steamboat

The waters run down, but man is not content
To walk or float, to travel where he's sent :
He has dreams, believes some destiny manifest
Up the river as well as down, and so the keelboats

Land, Light, Wind and Water

Followed weary backs up thousand miles of river
For many years until Fulton and others realized
Engines drawing water from mines
Could also draw mines up and down the waters.
Gold perfected the mountain boats --
Gold to be found, gold to be made --
The shallow draft, narrow-hulled paddle-pushed barges
With their plantation architecture over cable-slung frame.
It was Pittsburgh steel and Pennsylvania engineers
Built mountain boats at Brown's Ferry.
Built by water, many waters from their labors.
Montana furs and gold propelled and bound them.
Sent them out on pilgrimage from the far orient.

First down, down --
Down rivers with names like native heroes,
Monongahela, Allegheny, Ohio
Past the Muskingum, the Kanawha, the Guyandotte,
Past the Sandy and Scioto and Licking --
Past the Miami, the Kentucky, the Salt,
Past the Green and Wabash and Saline --
To the Mississippi, father of waters.
Then up, up --
Past the Big Muddy, past the Kaskaskia,
Past the Maramec to the mouth of the Missouri.
The Missouri, the muddy river, longest in the world
From its Rockies sources to the Gulf of Mexico:
The road to the West, with St. Louis as its gateway.
Up the Missouri, up past the Gasconade,
Up past the Osage, the Salt, the Blackwater,
Up past the Chariton, the Grand, and the Kansas,
Up past the Platte, the Nodaway, the Tarkio,
Up past the Boyer, the Little Sioux, the Floyd
Named for the one dead Lewis-Clark land-crosser,

Land, Light, Wind and Water

Up past the Big Sioux, the James, the Niobrara,
Up past White River, Medicine and Crow Creeks,
Up past the Bad, Okojobo, Cheyenne,
Past the Moreau, the Cannonball beyond the Grand,
The Heart, the Knife, the Little Missouri,
Shell Creek, White Earth, Little Muddy Creek, too.
Up past Yellowstone, Big Muddy, Poplar,
Up past Redwater, Porcupine, Milk River,
Musselshell, Judith, Marias and Teton.
There the journey ended -- the head of navigation,
Across from Shonkin Creek at the place named Fort
    Benton.
There furs were gathered, furs from the mountains,
Furs from the streams, until gold replaced them.
Gold from the streambed, gold from the mountains,
Flowed to load the steamboats, bought them in one
    season.
And the boats returned, enrichening the merchants
Of St. Louis, New York, London and Paris,
Down past the bison, down with the waters,
Down past the elk and the whitetail deer drinking,
Down past the white rocks, the monuments to no man,
Where the bighorn sheep climbed and the hoary marmot.

Beaver slapped and dove, their kindreds' pelts passing,
Eagles rose from cliff-tops, swallows swirled from faces,
Snakes stirred upon the rocks, rodents scurried under
Overhanging sandstone, hearing boiler thunder.

And the steamboat walked over the surface of the water
Up and down for sixty years, but when it died
It died truly, there was no resurrection,
And its converts among the natives, at least,
Were robbed of everything they owned,

Land, Light, Wind and Water

Given things they could not lose :
Smallpox, cholera and German measles.
But not just these, or white man's clothes --
No, -- white men, too, sold souls to steamboats
And trains that followed chaining
Their lives inextricably to the soul-sucking east ;
Which gave nothing of itself but us --
Not a cup of cold water. The waters, too, before
And after time of steamboats, ran ever east,
East and away -- never drying up.

XXIII. Aquatic Origins

The scientific scuttlebutt says our neck of the woods,
The wide region of these northern plains, was once an ocean,
A vast inland lake full of ancient aboriginal creatures.
And there are some signs something like that is true:
Alkali universally spread throughout the soil of our dry
    county ;
The nearly miraculous appearance once a blue moon,
When the summer's very wet, of strange fossil animals
In prairie ponds and wallows: notostracans or tadpole
    shrimp,
And clamshell shrimp and fairy shrimp,
Born apparently out of dust -- the same dust however,
That bears them over and over again, perhaps once lake
    bottom.
And if our land has aquatic origins, why not its people ?
It does not seem too much for our reeling minds to bear,
That we came about gradually from a water-cell somewhere.

Land, Light, Wind and Water

But why believe either thing? What's the point ?
There are no thought police driving our dusty roads.
Why not go back to the older account, at least give it credit
For explaining the phenomena ? --
An original world full of water, until God lined out land,
And another universal flood drowning all in its arc.
Those are questions of faith -- of two faiths.

We'd rather concern ourselves with recent history and
        thoughts
Of aquatic origins as they bear on our place
And our time and our problems as we have become.
Water, says Wallace Stegner, is the West's great weakness,
Because there is no water, the west will never be
What the east is (and some thank God for that).
Since this is a kind of doom we won't grow much beyond,
Our origins and character have to do with thirst as well as
        drinking.

Every settlement that springs up, that does not wither
On these plains and mountains, originates with water --
Water to drink, to water the stock, to wash with and grow by,
Or to use in industry, to cool with, to clean with,
Yes -- and to waste into.

A man can go forty days without food, they say,
But not without water --
If he does not have his tongue baptized,
He is soon headed for a devil-dazed hell.
His blood, evangelical evolutionists point out,
Consists mostly of water, with just as much salt
As his reputed old home the sea.
Furthermore the artists, the poets, the writers,
The myths belonging to Blackfoot and Gros Ventre,

Crow and Sioux, Kootenai and Salish,
Grow out of the water, out of the rivers, out of the lakes --
Still they are growing -- with roots on the banks
Their leaves floating downward.

The species owes its origins if not to aquaculture
Then to the Spirit moving on the face of the waters :
Our land, our towns, our hopes (some of our fears)
Were born of water, and in blood --
Carry our hope back to aquatic origins,
To a drinking and washing place still flowing.

XXIV. River as Cynic

The pathetic fallacy is here to stay --
What would you have me do, pretend ?
I tell you the river is a cynic as sure as I'm standing here
And I am standing here !
It's not an optimist -- although it runs on,
It's not a pessimist -- because it acknowledges no evil,
It's not a romantic -- because it neither feels or recollects,
And no modern nihilist -- though it be destructive.
The river is a cynic, it challenges all,
It asks personal questions of those come to call.

The river will not mind its manners,
It rejects convention, so that many a town or farm or boat
Especially lower down, changed sides over night --
Changed counties or states, or states of being

Land, Light, Wind and Water

From dryland to river bed, from water-borne to marooned.
Cynic -- dog-like -- notice how a dog noses up to anything
Like the river with a log, a raft, or a body,
Even a bluff, bridge, or boat -- nuzzling up and giving a
    shove
To see what it's about. Or lifting its leg to pee.
The river doubts, doubts seriously an argument's strength,
It says so right away, and goes to great length
To try it out, to test it, not satisfied with one reason,
Coming back with flood or drought, or ice in due season.
Lo and behold, the bluff, the rip-rap, the ferry
Does give way in time and the river makes merry,
Saying I told you so, I knew you were a front.
At times the river is more like a pack on a hunt
Than one dog, one cynic, as in spring break-up time,
When the river "goes out" and great blocks of ice grind,
Growl against banks and harry with skill,
With the current behind them and a penchant to kill.

The river is a cynic, but then cynics are trying
To find an unlikely truth to make life worth dying --
Truth that can stand up to intensest interrogation,
Truth that can part the waters and let pass a nation.

Land, Light, Wind and Water

XXV. *The Return*

Hello he said, remember me,
I've been four years upon the sea.
I've seen strange lands and I've seen strange men,
But the sea has brought me home again.

The sailor sighed: here in time's lea
Are there any lasses still walk free ?
What oceans hold my old friends' bones ?
What hillside bears my loved ones' stones ?

Good health and luck, the laddie said,
May the next tide take the tears you shed,
May your dreams be small so they can come true,
And may the sea run light for you.

XXVI. *Great Heart the Ocean*

You Great Heart, Ocean, pump your rich blood, life invisible
Across ethereal reaches to each blood-thirsty rock peak
And streambed of this flowing body,
Empty down upon the windswept limbs; each drinks of you
    and filled,

Overflows a channel, sends on and joins another,
Hastening together, brooks, streams, and rivers grow
In your branch-fed arteries, the myriad vessels of your body

Land, Light, Wind and Water

Carry liquid treasure down their clay courses each to each,
Sending and blending, meeting and diffusing,
Rolling stately at last to your wide embrace,
Many chambered mansions of your deep.

Marvelous invisible aeons of mist find flesh,
Fall inevitable to earth soil, soak and trickle.
Down fall the crystal drops, down the tiny veins
Issuing in streaming cuts on your mountain side,
Run along the barren crossings, ever saltier. Muddier, too,
With erosions of the world, streams still more thirsty,
Nearly desperate in their longing for the sweet mystery
Of purification, respiration, the respite of your breath.

A drop anonymous among so many seeps, flows, floods,
Channel to channel through the valves of time and is poured
    out,
Runs a while weeping, singing, slaking, until itself thirsty,
Dries on a plain, mud cracked under sun, broken to dust.
Where in earth's dried blood is tongue-cooling moisture ?
But tossed from your ceaseless waves, the drop becomes a
    mist,
Evaporation, something becomes nothing, tossed to the wind,
Dying distillation, clean into your moving.

The throbbing crash and roll of muscle, wave, and storm
Never starves the wanting cell.
The stream faints not in bed for want
Of healing drops prescribed, and given, perfectly
    administered,
Sharp wine poured out to end all thirst.

Heights stand vainly against your clouds, shed upon
    themselves

Your riven showers, nor can the dry earth in any extremity
Prevail to falter from your fierce flow, falling, making mud
    again,
Though dark dust rise in cataclysmic fall of mountains.

No cell or stream at last refuses rushing torrents --
No longer than your rushing winds, your turning tides allow.
None but you know when your pulse will speed, when slow
The lifeblood in its course to every, each well-known cell.
You alone know when your rain, mysterious sweet, shall fall
Midst thundered lightning down mountain sides once for all;
Flowing like blood and water, finally rush rumbling
To your vastness, the farthest and faintest, Source and
    stream,
Heart and cell, first and last will be one with
You Ever-flowing River, Heart and Headland,
Your waves and beaten body joined forever whole.

Lacrimae

Lord your eye undamming oer my sin
Pours out rain :
Aquifer coursing under a mountain,
River without banks,
Ocean without shores,
As from the torrents of your wounds,
Healing hastens from your
Unblinking eye.

Land, Light, Wind and Water

www.ingramcontent.com/pod-product-compliance
Lightning Source LLC
Chambersburg PA
CBHW022119040426
42450CB00006B/770